Piano • Vocal • Guitar

MORE 100 Years of Song
1900-1999

ISBN 0-634-00990-7

HAL•LEONARD®
CORPORATION
7777 W. BLUEMOUND RD. P.O. BOX 13819 MILWAUKEE, WI 53213

Visit Hal Leonard Online at
www.halleonard.com

More 100 Years of Song

More 100 Years of Song

Alphabetical Listing

ABOUT THE SONGS...
By Elaine Schmidt

Note: In many cases a song's popularity hit its peak in a year (or years, occasionally) after it was written.

A BIRD IN A GILDED CAGE
1900

Words by Arthur J. Lamb, Music by Harry Von Tilzer. This was one of the most successful of the sentimental ballads that were tremendously popular in the early 1900s. Von Tilzer agreed to set Lamb's lyric to music, but only if it was altered to make it clear that the unhappy woman the lyric described was a rich man's wife and not his mistress. Following its introduction – in a brothel, of all places (ironic, considering Von Tilzer's puritanical concerns) – the song sold more than two million copies of sheet music.

THE AMERICAN PATROL
1901

Music by F.W. Meacham. Although this march was written in the 1880s, it did not become a national favorite until John Philip Sousa's band recorded it in 1901. Sousa recorded it again during World War I, as did Charles Adam Prince's orchestra. Glenn Miller and his orchestra recorded their famous march/swing arrangement of the tune in 1942. It was also heard in the 1954 film *The Glenn Miller Story*.

ON A SUNDAY AFTERNOON
1902

Words by Andrew B. Sterling, Music by Harry Von Tilzer. Von Tilzer was on the beach one day when he heard someone say, "People work hard on Monday, but one day that's fun is Sunday." He talked Sterling into working the line into a song lyric. The result was one of Von Tilzer's most successful ballads, selling more than two million copies of sheet music in its first year alone. Von Tilzer and Sterling's song is not to be confused with the 1935 song of the same name by Arthur Freed and Nacio Herb Brown.

IN THE GOOD OLD SUMMERTIME
1903

Words by Ren Shields, Music by George Evans. One summer day in 1902, George Evans was dining with a few show business friends, when he made a remark in passing, saying that some people might like the winter, but he himself preferred the good old summertime. Singer Blanche Ring suggested that he write a song on the topic. She introduced it later that year in the musical *The Defender*. Publishers shied away from the tune, believing that seasonal songs would only sell during the three-month window of the season they described. "In the Good Old Summertime" broke that stereotype, keeping strong sales throughout the year.

GIVE MY REGARDS TO BROADWAY
1904

Words and Music by George M. Cohan. "Give My Regards to Broadway" was introduced by Cohan playing the title role in the 1904 musical *Little Johnny Jones*. It served as the title song in the 1948 film *Give My Regards to Broadway* and was heard in such films as *Yankee Doodle Dandy* (1942), *Jolson Sings Again* (1949), and *With a Song in My Heart* (1952). Cohan's famous tune remains the unofficial anthem of The Great White Way.

IN MY MERRY OLDSMOBILE
1905

Words by Vincent P. Bryan, Music by Gus Edwards. Just as bicycle songs had been popular in the heyday of the bike, automobile songs took over as cars appeared on American roads. "In My Merry Oldsmobile" was inspired by a cross country trip, from Detroit to Portland, Oregon, designed to publicize the Oldsmobile. The song became part of the commercial campaign. It was heard in the 1944 film *The Merry Monahans*, and was also used at various times in radio and television advertising for Oldsmobile.

I LOVE YOU TRULY
1906

Words and Music by Carrie Jacobs-Bond. "I Love You Truly" appeared in 1901 in a collection of art songs entitled *Seven Songs*. It did not become a hit until it was published as a single song in 1906, and crossed from art song to popular song. Bing Crosby recorded "I Love You Truly" in 1934 on the first disc released by the new Decca label. For decades the song was a standard at weddings. Beyond the wedding service, many brides and grooms throughout the country danced their first dance as a married couple to this song.

MY GAL SAL
1907

Words and Music by Paul Dresser. Also known as "They Called Her Frivolous Sal," this was Paul Dresser's last hit song. Dresser's career was in a shambles when he wrote it. His sentimental ballads were no longer in fashion, his fortunes had been frivolously spent, and he was discovering that his good friends were of the fair-weather variety. Dresser was certain he could still produce a hit, which he did. Unfortunately "My Gal Sal" sold more than two million copies, but only just after Dresser died.

CUDDLE UP A LITTLE CLOSER, LOVEY MINE
1908

Words by Otto Hauerbach, Music by Karl Hoschna. This was Otto Hauerbach's first hit. Not long after its success he altered his last name to the more American sounding "Harbach." Hauerbach and Hoschna intended the song for a vaudeville revue, but placed it in the operetta *The Three Twins* (1908) instead. The song was heard in several films, including *Birth of the Blues* (1941), *Coney Island* (1943), *Is Everybody Happy?* (1943), *The Story of Vernon and Irene Castle* (1939), and *On Moonlight Bay* (1951). It is heard as background music in the 1960 film *Tall Story*. Harbach went on to have a major songwriting career writing with several composers, producing hits such as "Smoke Gets in Your Eyes," "Indian Love Call," "Who?," and "Yesterdays."

BY THE LIGHT OF THE SILVERY MOON
1909

Words by Edward Madden, Music by Gus Edwards. Little Georgie Price, a child star in one of Gus Edwards' vaudeville revues, introduced this song in *School Boys and Girls*. Following a gimmick of the time, Price sang it while seated in the audience, under the pretense of an innocent cherub who expectedly bursts into song. That same year vaudeville star Lillian Lorraine sang in the *Ziegfeld Follies of 1909*. In 1933, after Ziegfeld's death, the Ziegfeld Theater was reopened. On opening night Gus Edwards brought Lillian Lorraine onto the stage and invited her to sing "By the Light of the Silvery Moon." She began the song, but broke into tears, overcome by nostalgia, and was unable to finish. This tune was one of the most featured songs in musical films of the 1940s and early '50s, when nostalgia for the early years of the century was in fashion. It was heard in the movies *The Story of Vernon and Irene Castle* (sung by Fred Astaire), *Birth of the Blues* (performed by Guy Lombardo), *Babes on Broadway* (sung by Judy Garland), *Hello, Frisco, Hello* (sung by Alice Faye), *The Jolson Story* (sung by Al Jolson), and *Two Weeks in Love* (sung by Jane Powell). The hit song became a hit movie in 1952's *By the Light of the Silvery Moon*, starring Doris Day.

MEET ME TONIGHT IN DREAMLAND
1910

Words by Beth Slater Whitson, Music by Leo Friedman. Whitson and Friedman made almost nothing from the two million copies of sheet music sold of this song. Their publisher, Leo Rossiter, had bought the song's rights outright and thus owed the songwriters nothing. Rossiter's brother Will opened a rival publishing house in 1910, promising to pay royalties to songwriters. Whitson and Friedman took their next ballad to him and made a fortune from that song, entitled "Let Me Call You Sweetheart." "Meet Me Tonight in Dreamland" was revived in the 1949 film *In the Good Old Summertime*, sung by Judy Garland.

PUT YOUR ARMS AROUND ME, HONEY
1911

Words by Junie McCree, Music by Albert Von Tilzer. It was introduced to vaudeville audiences in 1910 by singer/dancer Blossom Seeley. The song was heard in the 1944 film *Louisiana Hayride* (performed by the queen of the B musical, Judy Canova), and sung by Judy Garland in the 1949 film *In the Good Old Summertime*. "Put Your Arms Around Me, Honey" was given an unlikely revival in 1961 by "Fats" Domino.

MY MELANCHOLY BABY
1912

Words by George A. Norton, Music by Ernie Burnett. Burnett turned out to be a one-hit wonder with this tune. In fact, he may not have written the song at all. Heard in such films as *The Birth of the Blues* (1941) and *A Star Is Born* (1953), the song has been in legal dispute several times. In 1940 Burnett's former wife, Maybelle E. Watson, went to court alleging that she had written the song's lyric. She won damages on back royalties. In 1965 the song was back in court as Alan Light, son of songwriter Ben Light, alleged that his father had written this song but never taken credit for it.

PEG O' MY HEART
1913

Words by Alfred Bryan, Music by Fred Fisher. It first appeared in the *Ziegfeld Follies of 1913*. It was inspired by a successful Broadway comedy of the same name that had opened a year earlier. The song was dedicated to legendary actress Laurette Taylor, who had starred in the Broadway production. "Peg O' My Heart" served as the title song for a 1933 film, and was heard in the 1949 film *Oh, You Beautiful Doll*. The Harmonicats recorded it in 1947, selling over a million records.

BALLIN' THE JACK
1914

Words by Jim Burris, Music by Chris Smith. This ragtime dance piece was introduced in vaudeville by Billy Kent and Jeanette Warner in 1913. The lyric offers no clue as to the meaning of the phrase "ballin' the jack." Eddie Cantor sang it in vaudeville, making it a staple of his repertoire. When "Ballin' the Jack" was heard in the 1942 film *For Me and My Gal*, sung by Judy Garland, it landed on the Hit Parade. Danny Kaye sang the song for years and included it in the film *On the Riviera* (1951). Chubby Checker popularized a twist-styled version of the song.

THEY DIDN'T BELIEVE ME
1915

Words by Michael E. Rourke (Herbert Reynolds), Music by Jerome Kern. "They Didn't Believe Me" appeared in Jerome Kern's first successful musical, *The Girl from Utah* (1914). This was also the first Kern song to become a pop standard. According to legend, when Kern played this song for Victor Herbert, the elder songwriter is said to have commented, "This man will inherit my mantle." More than one historian has cited "They Didn't Believe Me" as the first song in the backbeat, fox trot ballad style. Because of this fresh American musical style, Kern was the model for many songwriters growing up at the time, including George Gershwin and Richard Rodgers.

I LOVE A PIANO
1916

Words and Music by Irving Berlin. Composer Irving Berlin really did love a piano – the one that allowed him to play in various keys. Berlin, an incomparable songwriter, was an extremely limited pianist who could not put his own music on paper. He used a transposing piano, which shifted keys via a large lever that actually moved the keyboard. Berlin referred to the piano as "the Buick." "I Love a Piano" was heard on stage in *Stop! Look! Listen!* (1915), and became popular around the country the next year. Judy Garland and Fred Astaire revived it memorably in *Easter Parade* (1948). The original lyric included the phrase "when Padarewski comes this way." Later, when that piano virtuoso was no longer as well-known, Berlin revised the line to "not only music from Broadway."

FOR ME AND MY GAL
1917

Words by Edgar Leslie and E. Ray Goetz, Music by George W. Meyer. One of the biggest sheet music sellers of 1917, topping three million copies, this song was just another day at work for composer George W. Meyer. "I sat down to and went to work," he said when talking about the song years later. "There was nothing remarkable about it. I was writing songs for a living and I needed the money so I wrote the ballad." Such famous performers as Sophie Tucker, Eddie Cantor, George Jessel and Al Jolson all put the song in their repertoires. Gene Kelly made his movie debut in *For Me and My Gal* (1942), and sweetly crooned the title song with Judy Garland. Their duet became a hit record.

THE CAISSONS GO ROLLING ALONG
1918

Words and Music by Edmund L. Gruber. The songwriter was a West Point graduate, class of 1904. Gruber wrote the song in 1908, while serving in the Artillery Corps of the U.S. Army. It remained fairly obscure until John Philip Sousa arranged it for band in 1918, calling it "U.S. Field Artillery March." The spirit of patriotism engendered by World War I helped launch Sousa's recording of the song that year. After he introduced his arrangement at a Liberty Loan concert at the Hippodrome in 1918, he was incorrectly credited as its composer for several years.

AFTER YOU'VE GONE
1919

Words by Henry Creamer, Music by Turner Layton. "After You've Gone" was popularized by Al Jolson on Broadway and by Sophie Tucker in vaudeville. After its first success in 1919, the song surfaced again in 1929 as the first New York hit for jazz great Louis Armstrong. It became a specialty of Benny Goodman, who played it on the soundtrack of the 1946 film *Make Mine Music*. The song has appeared in several other films, including *Unholy Partners* (1941), *For Me and My Gal* (1942), *Atlantic City* (1944), and the 1958, Frank Sinatra, Dean Martin and Shirley MacLaine film *Some Came Running*. Judy Garland's highly stylized arrangement, featured on her landmark Carnegie Hall album, is the performance that keeps the song alive.

WHISPERING
1920

Words and Music by Richard Coburn, Vincent Rose and John Schonberger. "Whispering" was popularized by Paul Whiteman and his orchestra, in a recording that sold more than a million copies. Now a pop standard, the song was heard in such films as *Ziegfeld Girl* (1941), *Greenwich Village* (1944), *Give My Regards to Broadway* (1948), *Belles on Their Toes* (1952), and *The Eddie Duchin Story* (1956).

LOOK FOR THE SILVER LINING
1921

Words by B.G. DeSylva, Music by Jerome Kern. It was written for a musical, *Brewster's Millions*, that never made it to Broadway. The song was salvaged and recycled in the musical *Good Morning Dearie* (1919). But it wasn't until it was sung by Marilyn Miller, the biggest theater star of her day, in the musical *Sally* (1920) that the song became popular. By 1921 it was a hit across the country. It later appeared in the film version of *Savoy* (1929), and in the film biography of Jerome Kern, *Till the Clouds Roll By* (1946). "Look for the Silver Lining" was also the title song for the 1949 film biography of Marilyn Miller.

APRIL SHOWERS
1922

Words by B.G. DeSylva, Music by Louis Silvers. Al Jolson was one of the greatest entertainers of the twentieth century. His individual style and sound, and his desperate need to please an audience created legendary performances. Jolson introduced "April Showers" in the stage musical *Bombo*. The song was an instant hit. He made "April Showers" a fixture of his act for many years, scoring a hit record with it as late as 1946 during his "come-back" period. He sang it on the soundtracks of the films *The Jolson Story* (1946) and *Jolson Sings Again* (1949).

TOOT, TOOT, TOOTSIE! (GOODBYE!)
1923

Words and Music by Ted Fiorito, Robert A. King, Gus Kahn, and Ernie Erdman. In 1922 Al Jolson was appearing on Broadway in the musical *Bombo*. When he came across a new song, "Toot, Toot, Tootsie, Goodbye," he decided to try it out by interpolating it into the show. The new song stopped the show. He recorded it almost immediately. When sound was added to what was previously only silent film, this was the first song ever heard in the movies, the first number sung by Jolson in *The Jazz Singer* (1927). He sang it again in *Rose of Washington Square* (1939). Doris Day performed it in the film biography of Gus Kahn, *I'll See You in My Dreams* (1951).

CALIFORNIA, HERE I COME
1924

Words by Al Jolson and B.G. DeSylva, Music by Joseph Meyer. By 1924 Al Jolson was on the road with the musical extravaganza *Bombo*. He interpolated "California, Here I Come" into the show while touring, and as he had done with other songs in this period, he launched another hit. He later sang it in the film musical *Rose of Washington Square* (1939). Jolson re-recorded the song in 1946, selling a million records. He also sang the number on the soundtracks of *The Jolson Story* (1946), and *Jolson Sings Again* (1949). The song has been heard in several other films, including *Lucky Boy* (1929) and *With a Song in My Heart* (1952). It was even heard in an episode of "I Love Lucy," sung by Lucy, Ricky, Fred and Ethel as they drive across the country to Los Angeles.

MANHATTAN

1925

Words by Lorenz Hart, Music by Richard Rodgers. "Manhattan" was the first hit for the legendary song-writing team of Rodgers and Hart, though they had been writing together for seven years by this time. It was the song that saved them. Rodgers was just about to give up on songwriting as a career when *The Garrick Gaieties* was an unexpected hit. The revue was originally just a two-performance benefit, but was so successful that a commercial Broadway run was quickly launched. The sophisticated "Manhattan," the hit from the show, took New York and the rest of the country by storm, encouraging Rodgers and Hart in an amazing career that would continue until Hart's death in 1943. The song was interpolated into several films, including the 1948 film biography (ridiculously fictionalized) of Rodgers and Hart entitled *Words and Music*. The song was also heard in other films such as *All About Eve* (1950), *With a Song in My Heart* (1952), *Don't Bother to Knock* (1953), and *The Eddie Duchin Story* (1956).

FIVE FOOT TWO, EYES OF BLUE

1926

Words by Sam M. Lewis and Joe Young, Music by Ray Henderson. This song is the epitome of a flapper era hit. It is so closely associated with the Roaring Twenties that it often appears in television and movie scenes depicting the era. "Five Foot Two, Eyes of Blue" was one of the early successes of Ray Henderson, before he began writing songs with Buddy DeSylva and Lew Brown. The tune has had a life long past its original success in 1926. Art Mooney and his Band made a successful recording of it in 1948. It turned up again in such films as *Has Anybody Seen My Girl* (1952), and *Love Me Or Leave Me* (1955).

BLUE SKIES

1927

Words and Music by Irving Berlin. Belle Baker introduced "Blue Skies" as an interpolation into the show *Betsy* (1927). The show's score had been written by Rodgers and Hart. Without telling the young songwriting team, the day before the opening she persuaded Irving Berlin she needed a hit to make a success of the musical. Her idea paid off, though it miffed Rodgers and Hart at the time. "Blue Skies" became the hit of the show. Al Jolson sang it in *The Jazz Singer* (1927) and dubbed it for Larry Parks in the 1946 film *The Jolson Story*. Eddie Cantor sang it in *Glorifying the American Girl* (1929); Ethel Merman and Alice Faye took a turn at it in *Alexander's Ragtime Band* (1938). Bing Crosby sang it in *Blue Skies* (1946) and *White Christmas* (1954). In 1978 the song was revived by country singer Willie Nelson.

I CAN'T GIVE YOU ANYTHING BUT LOVE

1928

Words by Dorothy Fields, Music by Jimmy McHugh. One day Fields and McHugh paused while walking past Tiffany's in New York. They overheard a young man tell his sweetheart, "Gee, honey, I can't give you nothin' but love." The resulting song, "I Can't Give You Anything But Love" was written for the 1927 Broadway revue *Delmar's Revels*. Although the show closed after just two weeks, the song turned up again in the revue *Blackbirds of 1928*. Cliff "Ukelele Ike" Edwards had the first hit record of this song, followed years later by jazz greats Louis Armstrong and Benny Goodman. The lyrics took on a new meaning during the Great Depression. Katherine Hepburn sang a bit of it in *Bringing Up Baby* (1938) and it served as the title song for a 1940 film. The song appeared in *True to the Army* (1942), *Stormy Weather* (1943), and *Jam Session* (1944). Gloria De Haven sang it in French in *So This Is Paris* (1955). By 1965 this song had been recorded nearly 450 times, Judy Garland's breathlessly slow rendition being one of the most memorable. Dorothy Fields was one of the only women able to break into the male dominated world of Tin Pan Alley as a songwriter.

MORE THAN YOU KNOW

1929

Words by Edward Eliscu and William (Billy) Rose, Music by Vincent Youmans. It would be easier to list the major vocalists of the 1930s-1950s who did not record this song than those who did. Although "More Than You Know" first appeared in the Broadway musical *Great Day* (1929), which ran only 36 performances, it found a second life in the hands of singer Jane Forman, who made the song one of her specialties. It appeared in such films as *Hit the Deck* (both the 1930 and 1955 versions), *The Helen Morgan Story* (1957), and in *Funny Lady* (1975), sung by Barbra Streisand.

PUTTIN' ON THE RITZ

1930

Words and Music by Irving Berlin. It was introduced by Harry Richman, in his screen debut, in the 1930 film *Puttin' on the Ritz*. Clark Gable uncharacteristically sang and danced to this song in the 1939 movie *Idiot's Delight*, a performance excerpted into the 1974 compilation film *That's Entertainment*. "Puttin' on the Ritz" was sung by Fred Astaire, with a revised lyric, in the 1946 film *Blue Skies*, a complex scene that showed him dancing in front of an eight-man chorus of Fred Astaires. Many other artists recorded the song. "Puttin' on the Ritz" was featured in the 1974 film *Young Frankenstein*, with Gene Wilder and Frankenstein singing and dancing in top hats and tails. The Dutch-Indonesian singer Taco had a disco-styled hit with it in 1983.

JUST A GIGOLO

1931

Words by Irving Caesar (English), Julius Brammer (German), Music by Leonello Casucci. "Just a Gigolo" was a hit in Vienna as "Schöner Gigolo" before Vincent Lopez and his orchestra popularized it in the U.S. with an English lyric. Bing Crosby recorded it soon after it became popular. The song was heard in the 1946 film *Lover, Come Back*. Some twenty years later Louis Prima and his band re-popularized it in a recording, coupling it with "I Ain't Got Nobody." David Lee Roth revived it in 1985.

HOW DEEP IS THE OCEAN
(HOW HIGH IS THE SKY)

1932

Words and Music by Irving Berlin. After he finished work on this song Berlin set it aside, thinking it was not one of his best efforts. It was several years before it was published. When the public finally heard it, it became one of the top hits of 1932. Among the many artists to record the song were Ethel Merman, Paul Whiteman and his orchestra, Joan Edwards, Coleman Hawkins, Dick Haymes, Benny Goodman, Margaret Whiting and Artie Shaw. Bing Crosby sang it in the 1946 film *Blue Skies* and Frank Sinatra performed it in *Meet Danny Wilson* (1952). In recent decades it's become a jazz standard.

DID YOU EVER SEE A DREAM WALKING?

1933

Words by Mack Gordon, Music by Harry Revel. One of the most characteristic of Depression era movie songs, it was introduced by Jack Haley in the 1933 film *Sitting Pretty*. Eddy Duchin, with vocal by Lew Sherwood, scored a number 1 hit record with the song. Other notable recordings include Guy and Carmen Lombardo, Bing Crosby, Meyer Davis and his orchestra, and The Pickens Sisters. It was prominently heard in the stylized Steve Martin 1981 film *Pennies from Heaven*, set in the 1930s.

SMOKE GETS IN YOUR EYES

1934

Words by Otto Harbach, Music by Jerome Kern. "Smoke Gets in Your Eyes" was a regular showstopper in the musical *Roberta* (1933), where it was introduced by Tamara. Two years later Fred Astaire and Ginger Rogers danced to it in the 1935 film adaptation of the show. Many years later Astaire recalled that the number had always been one of his favorites. Kern actually wrote this melody as a march, intending to use it as the theme song for a radio show. The radio show never made it to the air, but when the musical *Roberta* needed a new tune for the second act, Kern resurrected this song and slowed it down. He referred to "Smoke Gets in Your Eyes" as one of his favorite compositions, just as Harbach thought of it as some of his best work. The Platters' distinctive arrangement went to number 1 in 1959.

MY ROMANCE

1935

Music by Lorenz Hart, Music by Richard Rodgers. It was first heard in the 1935 musical *Jumbo*, a spectacle combining musical comedy and the circus. Rodgers and Hart had been on contract in Hollywood and hated it. *Jumbo* was their return to Broadway. The show, with actual circus acts, was such an elaborate spectacle that it took months of rehearsal. It always irked Rodgers that the producer, Billy Rose, wouldn't allow the songs from the show to be played on the radio during the rehearsal period or run. The song was heard in the 1963 film *Jumbo* (Rose had insisted on the title *Billy Rose's Jumbo*), and *Brotherly Love* (1970). The song is firmly in the jazz repertoire.

THE WAY YOU LOOK TONIGHT

1936

Words by Dorothy Fields, Music by Jerome Kern. It could be argued that more great songs were written for Fred Astaire by the top songwriters than any other performer. *Swing Time* (1936) was one of the nine great Astaire-Rogers musicals of the 1930s, and his best solo in it is "The Way You Look Tonight." Dorothy Fields had an urbane, casual way with a lyric that loosened up the usually more highbrow Kern. The song won an Academy Award. It has never left the repertoire, with hundreds of recordings. The classic was prominently featured in the 1997 Julia Roberts romantic comedy *My Best Friend's Wedding*.

CARAVAN

1937

Words by Irving Mills, Music by Juan Tizol and Edward Kennedy "Duke" Ellington. "Caravan" was introduced by Duke Ellington and his orchestra, in a performance that featured co-composer Juan Tizol on valve trombone. Billy Eckstine had a hit record with this song in 1949. It hit the charts again in 1953 in a recording by Ralph Marterie.

THANKS FOR THE MEMORY

1938

Words by Leo Robin, Music by Ralph Rainger. "Thanks for the Memory" will always be remembered as Bob Hope's theme song. He introduced it in his screen debut in the 1938 film *The Big Broadcast*. It's a bittersweet, witty duet, sung at the rail of the ocean liner Gigantic with Shirley Ross (playing his ex-wife). Years later he recalled in his autobiography, "[It] was the only number that kept me in pictures when I finished work on my first film. For that matter, it was only the most important song in my life." The song won an Academy Award in 1938 and was a hit record. It's a great example of the sophisticated, self-deprecating wit of the best of the songs of the 1930s. Songs like this were rarely written for the movies, which demanded a more populist approach. Hope's success with the song inspired Paramount to star him in the 1938 film *Thanks for the Memory*. "Thanks for the Memory" is such a well-crafted, intriguing song that it deserves a life of its own, and not just as Hope's theme song.

BEER BARREL POLKA

1939

Words by Lew Brown (English), Vasek Zeman and Wladimir A. Timm (Czech), Music by Jaromir Vejvoda. This most famous of polkas, one of the sheet music and record hits of 1939, is based on the Czech song "Skoda Lasky." It was first heard in the U.S. in the hands of Will Glahe and his Musette Orchestra. The Andrews Sisters soon had a hit record with it. The song was heard on stage in *Yokel Boy* (1939) and in the film *A Night in Casablanca* (1946). "Beer Barrel Polka" owed a good deal of its popularity to the new, streamlined version of the nickelodeon, known as the "juke box." An unusual, interesting use of the song is at every seventh-inning stretch for many years at the Milwaukee Brewers home games – Milwaukee being the unofficial polka capital of the U.S.

TUXEDO JUNCTION

1940

Words by Buddy Feyne, Music by Erskine Hawkins, William Johnson and Julian Dash. Erskine Hawkins and his band introduced this song as an instrumental at the Savoy Ballroom in New York City in 1939, recording it that same year. Named for an Alabama railroad junction, the song became a huge hit for Glenn Miller, and is one of the top Big Band numbers. The Andrews Sisters recorded it after lyrics were added. The song has been in the repertoire of The Manhattan Transfer since their 1973 debut album.

AQUELLOS OJOS VERDES (GREEN EYES)

1941

Words by E. Rivera and Eddie Woods (English), Adolfo Utrero (Spanish), Music by Nilo Menendez. This Cuban song was first heard in the U.S. in a performance by Don Azpiazu and his Havana Casino Orchestra. Jimmy Dorsey and his orchestra recorded it in 1941, with vocals by Bob Eberly and Helen O'Connell, scoring a number 1 hit and selling more than a million records. Dorsey, Eberly and O'Connell can be heard performing "Green Eyes" in the 1946 film *The Fabulous Dorseys*. With its Spanish lyric, the song has a completely different life as a standard of the Latin repertoire.

DON'T SIT UNDER THE APPLE TREE
1942

Words by Lew Brown and Charles Tobias, Music by Sam H. Stept. The familiar melody of "Don't Sit Under the Apple Tree" was originally attached to a lyric entitled "Anywhere the Bluebird Goes." It was introduced in the 1939 stage musical *Yokel Boy* with its "Apple Tree" lyric. The song soon became relevant after the U.S. entered World War II. It summed up the feelings of countless couples, who were separated by the war for several years, and was a particular favorite of service men and women. The Andrews Sisters sang it in the 1942 film *Private Buckaroo* and had a hit record with it that same year. Other best-selling recordings were made of "Don't Sit Under the Apple Tree" by Glenn Miller, Tex Beneke, and Kay Kyser.

THAT OLD BLACK MAGIC
1943

Words by Johnny Mercer, Music by Harold Arlen. The composer once explained this song's success, giving all the credit to Mercer's lyrics. "The words sustain your interest, make sense, contain memorable phrases and tell a story," he said. "Without the lyric, the song would be just another song." "That Old Black Magic" was a number 1 hit for Glenn Miller. It appeared in the films *Star Spangled Rhythm* (1942), *Here Come the Waves* (1944), *Radio Stars on Parade* (1945), *When You're Smiling* (1950), *Meet Danny Wilson* (1952), *Bus Stop* (1956), and *Senior Prom* (1958). Although such stars as Frank Sinatra, Sammy Davis, Jr., Bobby Rydell, and Louis Prima recorded the song, it was associated with Billy Daniels.

MAIRZY DOATS
1944

Words and Music by Milton Drake, Al Hoffman and Jerry Livingston. How successful was this nonsense song? For several weeks in a row after its release it sold some 30,000 copies of sheet music per day! When Milton Drake's little daughter came home from kindergarten one day saying "Cowzy tweet and sowzy tweet and liddle sharsky doisters," Milton had the idea for a song. He turned "Mares eat oats and does eat oats and little lambs eat ivy," into a runaway hit.

CANDY
1945

Words and Music by Mack David, Joan Whitney and Alex Kramer. This song went to number 1 on the charts in a recording by Johnny Mercer, Jo Stafford, and The Pied Pipers. It also did well in recordings by Dinah Shore, Johnny Long, and the Four King sisters performing with Buddy Cole's Orchestra. The Manhattan Transfer's tight vocal arrangement has been the version most often heard in recent decades.

ROUTE 66
1946

Words and Music by Bobby Troup. This hip road song was a hit for the King Cole Trio. Bing Crosby recorded it with the Andrews Sisters and had a success as well. Since that time the song has been part of the jazz standard repertoire. There's always been some bit of confusion about the "Route 66" song. The theme song for the 1962 television series is not the Troup song, but an instrumental by Nelson Riddle.

BEYOND THE SEA
1947

Words by Jack Lawrence (English), Music by Charles Trenet. The song first became popular in France in a recording by Trenet, entitled "La Mer." He also introduced it in the U.S. with the English lyric. Harry James, Benny Goodman and Mantovani all made popular instrumental recordings of this piece. Tex Beneke and his band recorded it with a vocal by Garry Stevens. Bobby Darin took a swingin' version of "Beyond the Sea" into the Top 10 in 1960.

BUTTONS AND BOWS
1948

Words and Music by Jay Livingston and Ray Evans. Bob Hope and Jane Russell introduced "Buttons and Bows" in the 1948 western comedy film *Paleface*. The song won an Academy Award, and was a best seller in a recording by Hope. Dinah Shore also recorded the song, selling more than a million records. A choral rendition was heard in the 1950 film *Sunset Boulevard*. Other hit versions were by The Happy Valley Boys, The Dinning Sisters, and Betty Garrett.

RIDERS IN THE SKY
1949

Words and Music by Stan Jones. Burl Ives introduced and recorded this song, but it was Vaughn Monroe and his Orchestra that popularized it with a million-selling recording. Peggy Lee had a hit recording, as did Bing Crosby. The song was revived by the Ramrods in 1961, The Baja Marimba Band in 1966, and The Outlaws in 1981. Also known as "A Cowboy Legend" or "Ghost Riders in the Sky," the song was sung by Gene Autry in the 1949 film *Riders in the Sky*.

MONA LISA
1950

Words and Music by Jay Livingston and Ray Evans. Although this was one of Nat King Cole's biggest hits, selling more than three million copies, he recorded it only after much persuasion. At first he thought a song on Leonardo da Vinci's masterpiece was a little too offbeat. The song was introduced in the 1949 film *Captain Carey, U.S.A.*, but only part of it was heard in the film and at that only in Italian. Still, it won an Academy Award. "Mona Lisa" was revived in 1959 by both rockabilly singer Carl Mann and country singer Conway Twitty.

CRY
1951

Words and Music by Churchill Kohlman. Johnnie Ray was one of the more stylized and over-the-top emotional singers of the early 1950s. Not only did Ray hit the charts with "Cry," he went to number 1, stayed there for almost three months, sold more than two million records and started a fashion for wailing ballads. The song was later revived by The Knightsbridge Strings (1959), Ray Charles (1965), Ronnie Dove (1966), Lynn Anderson (1972), and Crystal Gayle (1986).

YOUR CHEATIN' HEART

1952

Words and Music by Hank Williams. The songwriter had a hit record with this song, as did Joni James and Frankie Laine. "Your Cheatin' Heart" was one of the first country hits to have crossover appeal to a wider audience. Hank Williams Jr. performed "Your Cheatin' Heart" in the 1965 film biography of his dad. Such artists as Elvis Presley, Nat King Cole, Patsy Cline, Fats Domino, Jerry Lee Lewis, Petula Clark, and Leon Redbone also recorded the song.

I LOVE PARIS

1953

Words and Music by Cole Porter. Porter spent a significant amount of time in Paris in his life, and at least four of his musicals are set there. "I Love Paris" was inspired by the sumptuous sets created by Jo Mielziner for the stage musical *Can-Can* (1953). It was introduced in the show by Lilo. Frank Sinatra and Maurice Chevalier sang it in the film version of *Can-Can* (1960). The most popular recording of the song was made by Les Baxter and his Orchestra.

SHAKE, RATTLE AND ROLL

1954

Words and Music by Charles Calhoun. This was one of the earliest hits of the fledgling rock era. "Shake Rattle and Roll" was introduced by Joe Turner, who took it to number 22 on the charts in August of 1954. Bill Haley and his Comets had a million-selling record with it, taking it to number 7 that same month. The song was revived by Arthur Conley in 1967.

AUTUMN LEAVES

1955

Words by Johnny Mercer (English) and Jacques Prevert (French), Music by Joseph Kosma. After French singer Juliette Greco popularized "Les Portes de la Nuit" in Paris, Capitol Records contacted Johnny Mercer to write an English lyric for the song. Roger Williams' instrumental version of the song went to number 1 on the charts in 1955, selling more than a million records. Steve Allen, performing with the George Cates Orchestra, took it to number 35 on the charts. Jo Stafford, Monica Lewis, Stan Getz, and Tommy Mercer recorded the song as well. It was the title song for a nonmusical film starring Joan Crawford in 1956, sung on the soundtrack by Nat King Cole.

THE GREAT PRETENDER

1956

Words and Music by Buck Ram. The Platters were the most popular vocal group of the late 1950s, thanks in part to a string of enormously successful recordings that crossed over from the R&B/soul charts to the mainstream. "The Great Pretender" was one of the top ten songs of 1956, and a number 1 hit for the group. The Platters sang it in the 1957 film *The Girl Can't Help It*. The Platters were inducted into the Rock and Roll Hall of Fame in 1990.

ALL SHOOK UP

1957

Words and Music by Otis Blackwell and Elvis Presley. Elvis Presley was the first superstar of the rock era. His bedroom eyes, outlaw hips and swaggering mannerisms made him a sure hit with teens. Elvis' eclectic blues/country/gospel/rock style won him a crossover audience that came from every corner of the country. Nothing like Elvis had ever hit pop culture before. By the time "All Shook Up" hit number 1, where it stayed for eight weeks, Presley had already purchased Graceland with his hit record money. His huge stardom was a sure indication that rock was going to be around for awhile.

I CAN'T STOP LOVING YOU

1958

Words and Music by Don Gibson. When "I Can't Stop Loving You" first appeared, it charted as a crossover hit, starting on the country charts and then hitting the mainstream, recorded by Don Gibson. In 1962 Ray Charles recorded it in a soulful style, selling a million records and taking it to number 1. His version won a Grammy for Rhythm and Blues Song of the Year. Count Basie and his Orchestra recorded the song in 1963. Conway Twitty revived it in 1972.

KANSAS CITY

1959

Words and Music by Jerry Leiber and Mike Stoller. The up-tempo blues tune "Kansas City" first appeared in 1952 under the title "K. C. Lovin'." William Harrison took the "Kansas City" version to number 1 in 1959. Trini Lopez recorded the song in 1963, followed by James Brown in 1967.

IF EVER I WOULD LEAVE YOU

1960

Words by Alan Jay Lerner, Music by Frederick Loewe. The Broadway musical *Camelot* was based on the legends of King Arthur. Guenevere arrives at Camelot in an arranged marriage to Arthur, something she wants to run away from, until she meets the king and falls in love. Lancelot is a Frenchman who crosses the channel, lured by the tales of the high-minded Arthur and his knights of the round table. After a time, Lancelot and Guenevere fall in love. Guilty over their adulterous affair, Lancelot has grappled with thoughts of going away and ending it. But his real feelings are revealed in the song "If Ever I Would Leave You." Robert Goulet played Lancelot on Broadway, to Richard Burton's Arthur and Julie Andrews' Guenevere. The 1967 film version starred Richard Harris, Vanessa Redgrave, and Franco Nero.

RUNAWAY

1961

Words by Del Shannon, Music by Max Crook and Del Shannon. "Runaway" was Shannon's first hit, rocketing to number 1. He sang it again 25 years later, with an altered lyric, as the theme of the T.V. series *Crime Stories*. Bonnie Raitt took a revival of the song to the charts in 1977. The song contains one of the most famous instrumental interludes of the rock era.

I LEFT MY HEART IN SAN FRANCISCO
1962

Words by Douglass Cross, Music by George Cory. This song first appeared in 1952, introduced by Claramae Turner. It didn't make much of an impression. A decade later, sporting a new lyric, Tony Bennett and his musical director Ralph Sharon ran across the song, which had been submitted to them by the songwriters. "I Left My Heart in San Francisco" by Tony Bennett became one of the biggest hits of the year, selling about three million copies and winning a Grammy for Record of the Year. The song became his theme song, and the turning point in a career that he once said had been "all but ruined" by rock.

OUR DAY WILL COME
1963

Words by Bob Hilliard, Music by Mort Garson. This song was the only number 1 hit for an Akron rhythm & blues quintet known as Ruby and the Romantics. The group charted seven more times in the next two years, never again breaking into the top ten. Frankie Valli revived the song in 1975.

THE GIRL FROM IPANEMA
1964

Words by Norman Gimbel (English), Vinicius De Moraes (Portuguese), Music by Antonio Carlos Jobim. This Brazilian song, originally in Portuguese, was a hit record for saxophonist Stan Getz, with cool vocal styling by Astrud Gilberto (English) and Joao Gilberto (Portuguese). The Stan Getz Quartet gave the piece its U.S. introduction at the Café au Go Go in New York. When Jobim performed the song on Andy Williams' television show, it became a national hit. For a time in the mid-1960s, bossa novas were all the rage, and this is the song that started that craze. Ipanema is the name of a Brazilian beach.

YESTERDAY
1965

Words and Music by John Lennon and Paul McCartney. No one who ever saw Paul McCartney sing "Yesterday" on "The Ed Sullivan Show" will ever forget it. He tuned out all the screaming fans and sincerely, with a tear in his eye, sang this tender ballad of regret. It was one of The Beatles' biggest hits. It hit number 1 on the pop charts, winning the Ivor Novello Award in both 1965 and 1966. In the years since it became a hit, this song has been recorded more than 2500 times, making it one of the most recorded songs of all time.

MONDAY, MONDAY
1966

Words and Music by John Phillips. "Monday, Monday" was a number 1 hit for those lovable hippies the Mamas and the Papas. Although the group's lush vocal sound was California folk-pop and its members were connected with the Los Angeles psychedelic scene, their roots were in the Greenwich Village folk music community. The Mamas and the Papas had two years of great success, with six Top 5 hits in 1966 and '67. By '68 things had gone bad and the group disbanded, but not before becoming an icon of the flower-power era. They reunited briefly in 1971. "Mama" Cass Elliot went on to a solo career, but died in 1974. John Phillips, formerly of the Journeymen, was married to Michelle Phillips until 1970. She went on to an acting career, as did her daughter, MacKenzie Phillips.

HAPPY TOGETHER
1967

Words and Music by Garry Bonner and Alan Gordon. "Happy Together" was the biggest hit scored by the short-lived group The Turtles. The song was one of 1967's Top Ten records. The Turtles started out as The Nightriders, then changed their name to The Crossfires. The name changed to The Turtles in 1965 (in the wake of The Beatles, many groups adopted animal names). The band's personnel were never very stable, except for the core duo of Mark Volman and Howard Kaylan. The Turtles disbanded in 1970. Besides "Happy Together," their other hits were "Elenore," "It Ain't Me Babe," "She'd Rather Be with Me," "You Know What I Mean," and "You Showed Me." In 1987 the Nylons, a Canadian a cappella quartet, revived "Happy Together."

HEY JUDE
1968

Words and Music by John Lennon and Paul McCartney. Of all the hit singles The Beatles produced, this was the biggest. It was the number 1 record of the year and the best-selling single of the year. It spent more weeks on the pop charts than any other single of 1968, 19 weeks in all, and held the number 1 position for nine straight weeks. Their recording was also the longest single, at seven minutes and 11 seconds, played on American radio at the time, and the longest fade-out of any pop record, at about three minutes. Within another year, The Beatles had broken up for good, though the official announcement wasn't made until early 1970.

RAINDROPS KEEP FALLIN' ON MY HEAD
1969

Words by Hal David, Music by Burt Bacharach. The breezy, angular tunes of Bacharach and David have left an indelible mark on American pop music. They found a style of song that seemed classic and rooted to the standards era, but with the freshness of the rock era in them. "Raindrops Keep Fallin' on My Head" was introduced in the 1969 film *Butch Cassidy and the Sundance Kid*, winning an Academy Award. It was sung by B.J. Thomas in the film and on a recording that hit number 1.

YOUR SONG
1970

Words and Music by Elton John and Bernie Taupin. Elton John (born Reginald Kenneth Dwight) caught the attention of critics in 1970 in a performance that featured his original music, including "Your Song." But the music was only part of what made the news. Midway through the performance, John leapt to his feet, kicked the piano bench over and performed handstands on the piano. An act was born. "Your Song," which was on the artist's debut album, simply titled "Elton John," went to number 8 on the U.S. pop charts. It's somewhat of an unusual song in John's output; he's recorded relatively few love songs.

IT'S TOO LATE
1971

Words by Toni Stern, Music by Carole King. "It's Too Late" appeared on Carole King's enormously successful *Tapestry* album. Prior to the release of *Tapestry*, King was known primarily as a songwriter. With the album she made a name for herself as a performer as well. "It's Too Late" hit number 1 on the charts, winning a Grammy for Record of the Year.

ROCKY MOUNTAIN HIGH

1972

Words and Music by John Denver and Michael Taylor. "Rocky Mountain High," now the unofficial theme song of Colorado, was the title song of one of John Denver's four platinum albums. Twelve other Denver albums went gold. Following his death in a plane crash in 1997, Denver was hailed by Sony as one of the five top artists of all time. He was named Colorado's Poet Laureate in 1974, in great part on the basis of this song.

KILLING ME SOFTLY WITH HIS SONG

1973

Words by Norman Gimbel, Music by Charles Fox. Although this song was introduced by Lori Lieberman, it is Roberta Flack's number 1 recording that became a hit. Her rendition won a Grammy for Song of the Year and Record of the Year. In the 1990s, The Fugees scored a hit with a remake of the famous song.

DON'T LET THE SUN GO DOWN ON ME

1974

Words and Music by Elton John and Bernie Taupin. Long before international rock fans knew anything of Elton John and Bernie Taupin, the pair was churning out songs for other musicians. Taupin would write lyrics all day, sometimes at the rate of a song per hour. He would deliver packages of them to John who would immediately set them to music. When John began performing the tunes himself, it was with a flamboyant delivery that was compared to that of Jerry Lee Lewis. As all the world knows, John easily exceeded any previous artist's over-the-top style in his live concerts. He became the first act since The Beatles to have four albums in the American Top Ten at the same time. "Don't Let the Sun Go Down on Me" went gold for John, peaking at number 2 on the U.S. charts. A 1992 version recorded by Elton John and George Michael went to number 1.

CAN'T SMILE WITHOUT YOU

1975

Words and Music by Chris Arnold, David Martin and Geoff Morrow. Trained at Juilliard, Barry Manilow, who started out writing jingles, made a name for himself as a composer, arranger, performer, and producer. Early in his career he was Bette Midler's accompanist, and produced her first two albums. Manilow's pop songs of the '70s brought him international fame. After his first album went platinum, twelve more followed suit, including two that went multi-platinum. In 1977 Manilow had five albums on the charts at once, something accomplished only twice before, by Frank Sinatra and Johnny Mathis.

TONIGHT'S THE NIGHT

1976

Words and Music by Rod Stewart. When "Tonight's the Night," from Rod Stewart's *A Night on the Town* album, first hit U.S. airwaves it got late night play if at all. Across the country, radio program directors opted not to air the song, finding its lyric too sexually explicit. But public demand won out. Once the song was on the air it soared to number 1 on the charts.

HOW DEEP IS YOUR LOVE

1977

Words and Music by Barry Gibb, Maurice Gibb and Robin Gibb. The Gibb brothers, once poster boys for disco, have become one of the wealthiest groups in the pop industry. Sons of a British bandleader, the brothers have had an uncanny ability to sniff out trends and incorporate them into their ever-changing act. "How Deep Is Your Love," a disco ballad, was introduced on the soundtrack of *Saturday Night Fever*, with the single going gold almost immediately after the movie's release.

DUST IN THE WIND

1978

Words and Music by Kerry Livgren. Although dismissed by early critics as rehashed British progressive rock, the complex classic rock sound of Kansas was a hit with audiences. Formed in Topeka, Kansas, the band began by playing local clubs, with very limited success. The group's first two albums sold a few hundred thousand copies. But in 1977 their album *Leftoverture*, containing the hit "Carry On Wayward Son," sold more than three million copies. *Point of Know Return*, containing "Dust in the Wind," went triple platinum. "Dust in the Wind" hit number 6 on the charts. The mellow, acoustic sound of the recording is unlike most of the band's harder edged material.

Y.M.C.A.

1979

Words and Music by Henri Belolo, Jacques Morali and Victor Willis. The Village People, complete with overplayed stereotypes and double-entendre lyrics, were a joke that most of America didn't get. The obviously gay themes of their tunes went right past many of those who were dancing in the flashing lights of disco clubs. "Y.M.C.A." was a platinum record for the group. Although they faded from view in the U.S. by the early '80s, the group maintained a large international following for several years. "Y.M.C.A." is still one of the most popular party songs, and can be heard at nearly every major sporting event.

SAILING

1980

Words and Music by Christopher Cross. The singer-songwriter appeared on the national pop scene in 1980 with the album *Christopher Cross*. The album went quadruple platinum with four of its songs hitting the Top 20, including "Sailing." The song went to number 1. Cross won five Grammy Awards that year, including Album of the Year, Song of the Year, and Record of the Year. He had one more huge hit with "Arthur's Theme (The Best That You Can Do)" from the film *Arthur*, and a couple of other respectable singles before fading from view.

PHYSICAL
1981

Words and Music by Stephen Kipner and Terry Shaddick. "Physical," from Olivia Newton-John's album of the same name, was part of a deliberate image change for the once squeaky-clean singer. In 1974 Newton-John won Female Vocalist of the Year from the Country Music Association, which caused some members to quit in protest. In 1978 she appeared opposite John Travolta in *Grease*, the most profitable movie musical made to date. The image change she underwent in *Grease* carried over into her musical act. From that point on the world saw a sexier, rock-oriented Olivia. "Physical" hit number 1 on the charts, with the album going platinum. It was a notable video of its era, with Newton-John among a bunch of near naked gym hunks.

CHARIOTS OF FIRE
1982

Music by Vangelis. "Chariots of Fire," that inspirational anthem, was on the U.S. charts for 15 weeks. The instrumental composition was recorded by keyboardist/composer Vangelis (a pseudonym for Evangelos Odyssey Papathanassiou). Vangelis won an Academy Award for the score to *Chariots of Fire*, a film about two athletes striving for glory in the 1924 Olympic Games.

TIME AFTER TIME
1983

Words and Music by Cyndi Lauper and Rob Hyman. Cyndi Lauper hit the rock scene with a splash in 1983. Her debut album, *She's So Unusual*, had four Top Five singles, including "Time After Time." This was a first for a woman in the music industry. Lauper, sporting a childlike voice and a tattered, urban image, used the new medium of MTV to propel herself to stardom. Sometimes lost in the hubbub was her excellent songwriting, of which this song is a prime example. The jazz duo Tuck & Patti recorded a memorable rendition of "Time After Time," and more than most songs of the rock era, it has become a standard among performers in various styles. Inoj had a top-ten hit with a new rendition in 1998.

I JUST CALLED TO SAY I LOVE YOU
1984

Words and Music by Stevie Wonder. Before finding a second life in advertising for long distance telephone service, Stevie Wonder's "I Just Called to Say I Love You" was a number 1 hit. It's a cheerful love song, typical of Wonder's songwriting. The song was introduced in the 1984 film *The Woman in Red*. Wonder took home an Academy Award for the song, as well as a Grammy for Song of the Year.

WE BUILT THIS CITY
1985

Words by Bernie Taupin, Dennis Lambert, Martin Page and Peter Wolf, Music by Lambert, Page and Wolf. Introduced by Starship, on the platinum album *Knee Deep in the Hoopla*, "We Built This City" was a number 1 hit. Starship was the last incarnation of the long-lived rock franchise known first as Jefferson Airplane and later as Jefferson Starship. The only common denominator in these editions of the band was singer Grace Slick.

GLORY OF LOVE
1986

Words and Music by Peter Cetera, David Foster and Diane Nini. Former lead singer for the band Chicago, Peter Cetera set out on his own in 1985. The following year he scored a number 1 hit with "Glory of Love," and hit the charts with several other tunes. But his solo albums never hit the Top Twenty. This song, heard on the soundtrack of the film *Karate Kid II*, was nominated for an Academy Award and a Golden Globe. Cetera's distinctive, high voice seemed perfect for the romantic ballads he so often recorded.

I STILL HAVEN'T FOUND WHAT I'M LOOKING FOR
1987

Words and Music by U2. Known as one of the most adventurous and innovative acts in pop music, U2 had a number 1 hit with "I Still Haven't Found What I'm Looking For" from the album *The Joshua Tree*. Formed in Dublin, Ireland, the band was the most widely followed rock act of the '80s, making the cover of *Time* magazine in 1987. The group remained popular into the '90s, releasing the album *Pop* in 1997 and *Best of 1980-1990* in 1998.

KOKOMO
1988

Words and Music by Mike Love, Scott McKenzie, Terry Melcher and John Phillips. In the early '60s The Beach Boys epitomized California pop/rock. Now America's most famous nostalgia act, they have sold nearly 70 million records worldwide. The happy-go-lucky "Kokomo" was introduced in the Tom Cruise film *Cocktail* (1988), becoming a hit single. The Beach Boys were inducted into the Rock and Roll Hall of Fame in 1988.

UNDER THE SEA
1989

Words by Howard Ashman, Music by Alan Menken. The happy calypso song was written for the first animated blockbuster in the Disney renaissance. *The Little Mermaid* was the studio's first feature-length animated fairytale since 1959. "Under the Sea" won an Academy Award and a Golden Globe. Ashman and Menken made musical magic again, working together on Disney's *Beauty and the Beast* (1991). The pair wrote three songs for *Aladdin* (1992) before Ashman's untimely death ended their partnership.

HOW AM I SUPPOSED TO LIVE WITHOUT YOU
1990

Words and Music by Michael Bolton and Doug James. "How Am I Supposed to Live Without You" first charted in 1983, in a recording by Laura Branigan. She took the song to number 12 on the pop charts and number 1 on the adult contemporary charts. It wasn't until co-composer Michael Bolton recorded the song himself that it soared to number 1 on the pop charts.

SOMEDAY
1991

Words and Music by Mariah Carey and Ben Margulies. "Someday" appeared on Mariah Carey's 1990 debut album, *Mariah Carey*. The album brought rave reviews for the young singer and her incredible vocal range. Nearly all of Carey's subsequent singles have gone to the number 1 spot on the charts. In 1998 she even released an album entitled *#1's*, featuring "Someday" and other chart-topping hits.

END OF THE ROAD
1992

Words and Music by Babyface (Kenneth B. Edmonds), Antonio M. Reid and Daryl L. Simmons. Babyface emerged as the most important pop songwriter of the 1990s. His songs have become hits for such stars as Michael Jackson, Gladys Knight, Sheena Easton, Aretha Franklin, Paula Abdul, and Whitney Houston. "End of the Road," which was written for Boyz II Men, became one of the best-selling hits of all time. It surpassed Elvis Presley's "Heartbreak Hotel" in the length of its stay in the number 1 spot on the *Billboard* Hot 100 chart.

FIELDS OF GOLD
1993

Words and Music by Sting (a.k.a. Gordon Sumner). When Sting's band, The Police, was at the height of its success, Sting himself disbanded the group. Always antsy for a new challenge, Sting found success in recordings with jazz musician Branford Marsalis, appeared in numerous films and starred on a Broadway revival of *The Threepenny Opera*. His solo recording career has been a steady stream of hits. "Fields of Gold," from Sting's 1993 album *Ten Summoner's Tales*, was released again in 1994 as the title track of an anthology album.

CAN YOU FEEL THE LOVE TONIGHT
1994

Words by Tim Rice, Music by Elton John. Famous for his flamboyant costumes and keyboard-heavy rock music, Elton John found a new audience with Disney's animated feature *The Lion King*. Disney executives asked lyricist Tim Rice who his first choice would be as a songwriter. Rice responded, "Elton John would be fantastic." Disney's producers thought John would turn them down, but he jumped at the chance. His songs were an instant hit with the children at whom the movie was directed. "Can You Feel the Love Tonight" also appealed to adult listeners, making it to number 4 on the pop charts. This song won an Academy Award for Best Song.

EXHALE (SHOOP SHOOP)
1995

Words and Music by Babyface (Kenneth B. Edmonds). Singer Whitney Houston became a movie star in *The Bodyguard*, and her film career continued with *Waiting to Exhale*, the story of four African-American women and their search for love. The soundtrack album won an Image Award in 1996. "Exhale (Shoop Shoop)" was nominated for the MTV Movie Award for Best Movie Song, but the award went to "Sittin' Up in My Room," also from this film.

I FINALLY FOUND SOMEONE
1996

Words and Music by Barbra Streisand, Marvin Hamlisch, R.J. Lange and Bryan Adams. Streisand herself sang the song on the soundtrack to the film *The Mirror Has Two Faces*, a romantic comedy about two intellectuals who marry on the theory of friendship is best, but wind up falling in love. The song was nominated for an Academy Award and a Golden Globe. It won the A.S.C.A.P. Award for Most Performed Songs from Motion Pictures.

BUTTERFLY KISSES
1997

Words and Music by Robert Mason Carlisle and Randy Keith Thomas. "Butterfly Kisses" was a surprising crossover hit for country/gospel singer Bob Carlisle. Written as a love song to his daughter, it was released just before Father's Day on an album entitled *Shades of Grace*. When the song took off, the album was released again under the title *Butterfly Kisses*. The song won Carlisle a number of awards including a Grammy for Best Country Song, a Gospel Music Association Dove Award for Southern Gospel Recorded Song of the Year, and an American Music Award for New Country Artist.

YOU'RE STILL THE ONE
1998

Words and Music by Robert John Lange and Shania Twain. Born Eileen Regina Edwards, Shania Twain created her name using her stepfather's surname, Twian, and the Ojibway word meaning "I'm on my way." It took a few years for Nashville to warm up to Twain, with her glamour and pop influences. After her huge success on the pop charts, as well as the country charts, no one could question her place in Nashville anymore. The Canadian singer won numerous awards with this song, including Grammy Awards for Best Country Song and Best Country Vocal Performance, a Billboard Music Award for Best-Selling Country Single, a Blockbuster Entertainment Award for Favorite Single, and a BMI Pop Song of the Year Award.

YOU'LL BE IN MY HEART
1999

Words and Music by Phil Collins. Following in the successful footsteps of Elton John, rock musician Phil Collins took a turn at writing songs for Disney's animated feature *Tarzan*™, contributing five songs to the film. The former lead singer and drummer of the band Genesis, Collins scored an instant hit with "You'll Be in My Heart," and was presented with a star on the Hollywood Walk of Fame. He recorded the song in French, German, Italian and two dialects of Spanish, marking the first time that a Disney animated feature was released with international versions of songs by the same recording artist. Unlike previous Disney musicals where the characters sing the songs, Collins himself sings all the songs on the soundtrack.

1900
A Bird in a Gilded Cage

Words by ARTHUR J. LAMB
Music by HARRY VON TILZER

19

1901
The American Patrol

Music by F.W. MEACHAM

1902
On a Sunday Afternoon

Words by ANDREW B. STERLING
Music by HARRY VON TILZER

1903
In the Good Old Summertime
from IN THE GOOD OLD SUMMERTIME

Words by REN SHIELDS
Music by GEORGE EVANS

1904
Give My Regards to Broadway

Words and Music by
GEORGE M. COHAN

1905
In My Merry Oldsmobile

Words by VINCENT BRYAN
Music by GUS EDWARDS

1906
I Love You Truly

Words and Music by
CARRIE JACOBS-BOND

Moderate Waltz

tru - ly, dear. _____

Life with its

sor - rows, life

with its tears. _____

41

1907
My Gal Sal

Words and Music by
PAUL DRESSER

she was al - ways will - ing to

share. _____ A wild sort of

dev - il, but dead on the lev - el, was

my gal Sal. _____

1908
Cuddle Up a
Little Closer, Lovey Mine

from THE THREE TWINS

Words by OTTO HARBACH
Music by KARL HOSCHNA

1909
By the Light of the Silvery Moon

Lyrics by ED MADDEN
Music by GUS EDWARDS

1910
Meet Me Tonight in Dreamland

Words by BETH SLATER WHITSON
Music by LEO FRIEDMAN

1911
Put Your Arms Around Me, Honey

Words by JUNIE McCREE
Music by ALBERT VON TILZER

Night-time am a fall-in'
Mu-sic am a play-in'

ev-'ry-thing is still, and the moon am a shin-ing from a-
such a "lov-in' glide," that my feet keep a mov-ing to and

bove.
fro.

Cu-pid am a call-in'
And with you a sway-in'

1912
My Melancholy Baby

Words by GEORGE NORTON
Music by ERNIE BURNETT

Come sweet-heart mine, _
Birds in the trees, _

sun   shines   through.

Smile my hon - ey   dear,   while I   kiss a - way each

tear.   Or   else I   shall   be   mel - an - chol - y

too.   Now   won't   you   too.

1913
Peg O' My Heart

Words by ALFRED BRYAN
Music by FRED FISHER

1914
Ballin' the Jack

Words by JIM BURRIS
Music by CHRIS SMITH

1915
They Didn't Believe Me
from THE GIRL FROM UTAH

Words by HERBERT REYNOLDS
Music by JEROME KERN

1916
I Love a Piano
from the Stage Production STOP! LOOK! LISTEN!

Words and Music by
IRVING BERLIN

1917
For Me and My Gal

Words by EDGAR LESLIE and E. RAY GOETZ
Music by GEORGE W. MEYER

1918
The Caissons Go Rolling Along

Words and Music by
EDMUND L. GRUBER

1919
After You've Gone
from ONE MO' TIME

Words by HENRY CREAMER
Music by TURNER LAYTON

1920
Whispering

Words and Music by RICHARD COBURN,
JOHN SCHONBERGER and VINCENT ROSE

Hon - ey, I have some - thing to tell you
When the twi - light shad - ows are fall - ing

and it's worth - while lis - ten - ing to.
and the wea - ry world is at rest.

Put your lit - tle head on my shoul - der dear,
Then I'll whis - per just why I know

1921
Look for the Silver Lining
from SALLY

Words by BUDDY DeSYLVA
Music by JEROME KERN

glad - ness _____ Will al - ways ban - ish sad - ness and

strife _____ So al - ways look for _____ the sil - ver

lin - ing _____ And try to find the sun - ny side of

life.

life. _____

1922
April Showers
from BOMBO

Words by B.G. DeSYLVA
Music by LOUIS SILVERS

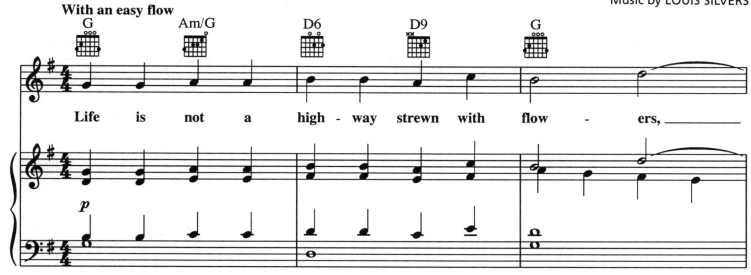

Life is not a high-way strewn with flow - ers, _____

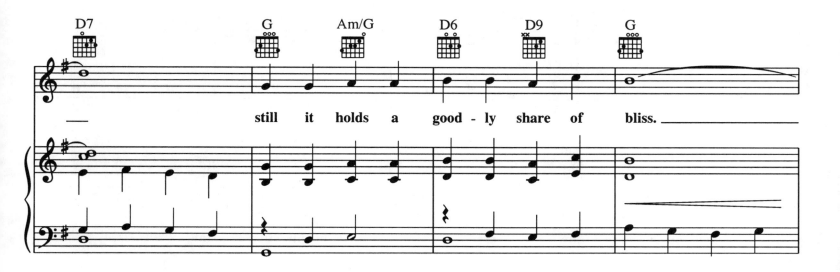

_____ still it holds a good - ly share of bliss. _____

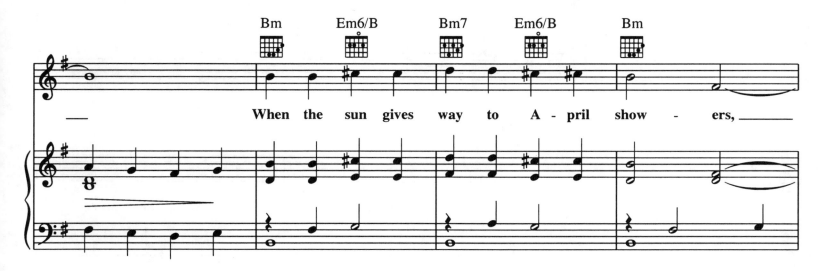

_____ When the sun gives way to A - pril show - ers, _____

1923
Toot, Toot, Tootsie!
(Good-bye!)

Words and Music by GUS KAHN, ERNIE ERDMAN,
DAN RUSSO and TED FIORITO

and sev - en times he hur - ried back to kiss his love a -
he seemed to take a lot of pleas - ure say - ing bye - bye

gain, and tell her:
to his treas - ure:
Toot, toot, Toot - sie, good - bye!

Toot, toot, Toot - sie, don't cry.

The choo choo train that takes

If you don't get a let-ter then you'll know I'm in jail.

Toot, toot, Toot-sie don't cry.

Toot, toot, Toot-sie good-

bye!

bye!

1924
California, Here I Come

Words and Music by AL JOLSON,
B.G. DeSYLVA and JOSEPH MEYER

1925
Manhattan
from the Broadway Musical THE GARRICK GAIETIES

Words by LORENZ HART
Music by RICHARD RODGERS

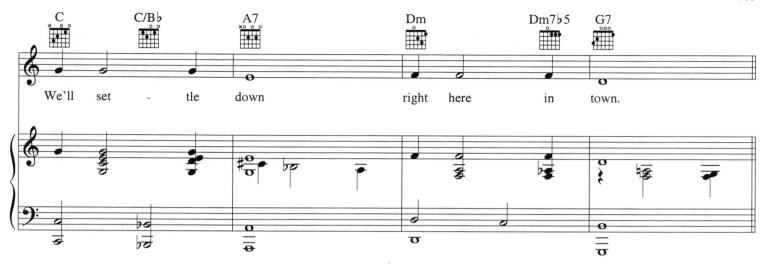

We'll set - tle down   right here   in   town.

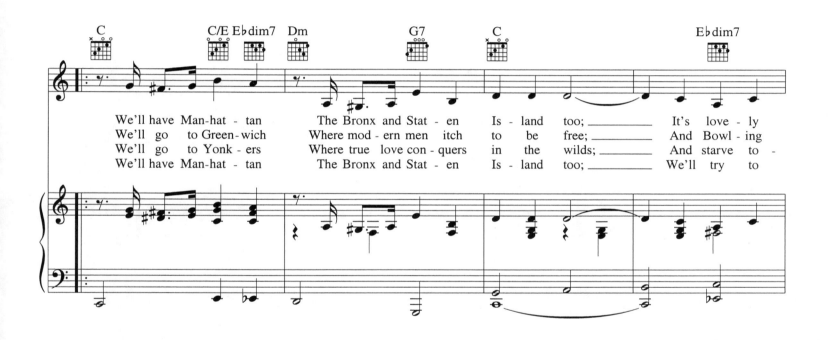

We'll have Man-hat - tan   The Bronx and Stat - en   Is - land   too; _____ It's love - ly
We'll go   to Green-wich   Where mod - ern men itch   to   be   free; _____ And Bowl - ing
We'll go   to Yonk - ers   Where true love con - quers   in   the   wilds; _____ And starve to -
We'll have Man-hat - tan   The Bronx and Stat - en   Is - land   too; _____ We'll try to

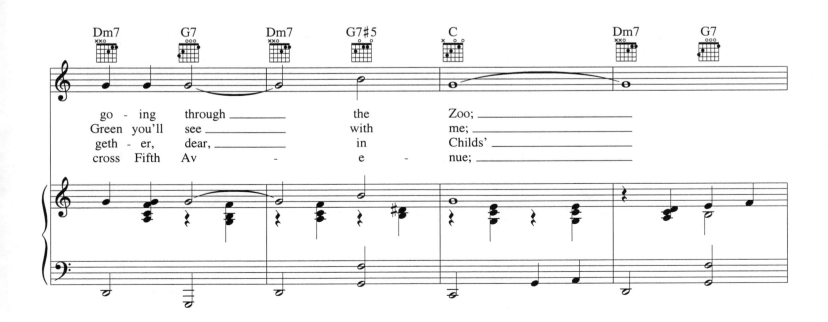

go - ing   through _____ the   Zoo; _____
Green you'll   see _____ with   me; _____
geth - er,   dear, _____ in   Childs' _____
cross Fifth Av - e - nue; _____

1926

Five Foot Two, Eyes of Blue

(Has Anybody Seen My Girl?)

Words by JOE YOUNG and SAM LEWIS
Music by RAY HENDERSON

1927
Blue Skies
from BETSY

Words and Music by
IRVING BERLIN

1928
I Can't Give You Anything but Love

from BLACKBIRDS OF 1928

Words by DOROTHY FIELDS
Music by JIMMY McHUGH

1929
More Than You Know

Words by WILLIAM ROSE and EDWARD ELISCU
Music by VINCENT YOUMANS

1930
Puttin' on the Ritz
from the Motion Picture PUTTIN' ON THE RITZ

Words and Music by
IRVING BERLIN

Have you seen the well-to-do__ up and down Park Av-e-nue,__ on that fam-ous thor-ough-fare__ with their nos-es in the air.__ High hats and

1931
Just a Gigolo

Original German Text by JULIUS BRAMMER
English Words by IRVING CAESAR
Music by LEONELLO CASUCCI

134

1932
How Deep Is the Ocean
(How High Is the Sky)

Words and Music by
IRVING BERLIN

1933
Did You Ever
See a Dream Walking?

from SITTING PRETTY

Words by MACK GORDON
Music by HARRY REVEL

1934
Smoke Gets in Your Eyes
from ROBERTA

Words by OTTO HARBACH
Music by JEROME KERN

1935
My Romance
from JUMBO

Words by LORENZ HART
Music by RICHARD RODGERS

1936
The Way You Look Tonight
from SWING TIME

Words by DOROTHY FIELDS
Music by JEROME KERN

1937
Caravan
from SOPHISTICATED LADIES

Words and Music by DUKE ELLINGTON,
IRVING MILLS and JUAN TIZOL

1938
Thanks for the Memory

from the Paramount Picture BIG BROADCAST OF 1938

Words and Music by LEO ROBIN
and RALPH RAINGER

1939

Beer Barrel Polka

(Roll Out the Barrel)

Based on the European success "Skoda Lasky"*

By LEW BROWN, WLADIMIR A. TIMM,
JAROMIR VEJVODA and VASEK ZEMAN

There's a gar - den what a gar - den on - ly
hap - py fac - es bloom there, and there's nev - er an - y
room there for a wor - ry or a gloom there. Oh, there's

mu - sic and there's danc - ing and a lot of sweet ro -

manc - ing. When they play a pol - ka they all get in the

swing. Ev - 'ry time they hear that oom - pa - pa,
hear a rum - ble on the floor,

ev - 'ry - bod - y feels so tra - la la.
it's the big sur - prise they're wait - ing for.

F   F7

Bb   F7

Bb

They want to throw their cares a - way,
And all the cou - ples form a ring,

they all go lah - de - ah - de - ay.
for miles a - round you'll

Then they hear them sing.

Roll out the bar - rel, we'll have a bar - rel of fun.

Roll out the bar - rel, we've got the blues on the run.

1940
Tuxedo Junction

Words by BUDDY FEYNE
Music by ERSKINE HAWKINS,
WILLIAM JOHNSON and JULIAN DASH

1941
Aquellos ojos verdes
(Green Eyes)

Music by NILO MENENDEZ
Spanish Words by ADOLFO UTRERA
English Words by E. RIVERA and E. WOODS

Life held no charm, dear, un-til I met you.

Fue- ron tus o-jos los que me die-rón

1942
Don't Sit Under the Apple Tree
(With Anyone Else but Me)

Words and Music by LEW BROWN,
SAM H. STEPT and CHARLIE TOBIAS

Don't sit un-der the ap-ple tree with an-y-one else but me,

an-y-one else but me, an-y-one else but me. No! No! No!

Just re-mem-ber that I've been true to no-bod-y else but you, so

just be true to me.

1943
That Old Black Magic

from the Paramount Picture STAR SPANGLED RHYTHM

Words by JOHNNY MERCER
Music by HAROLD ARLEN

1944
Mairzy Doats

Words and Music by MILTON DRAKE,
AL HOFFMAN and JERRY LIVINGSTON

1945
Candy

By ALEX KRAMER, JOAN WHITNEY
and MACK DAVID

1946
Route 66

By BOBBY TROUP

It winds _____ from Chi - ca - go to L. A., _____

more than two _____ thou-sand miles all the way._

Get your kicks on Route_ Six - ty Six!_

Now you go thru Saint Loo-ey Jop - lin, Mis-sour-i and

1947
Beyond the Sea

English Lyrics by JACK LAWRENCE
Music and French Lyrics by CHARLES TRENET

1948
Buttons and Bows
from The Paramount Picture PALEFACE

Words and Music by JAY LIVINGSTON
and RAY EVANS

1949
(Ghost)
Riders in the Sky
(A Cowboy Legend)
from RIDERS IN THE SKY

By STAN JONES

Moderately (in 2)

1. An old cow-boy went rid-ing out one dark and wind-y
2. (Their) brands were still on fi-re and their hooves were made of
3. (Their) fac-es gaunt, their eyes were blurred, their shirts all soaked with
4. (As the) rid-ers loped on by him, he heard one call his

day, _____
steel, _____
sweat, _____
name, _____

Up-on a ridge he
Their horns were black and
He's rid-in' hard to
"If you want to save your

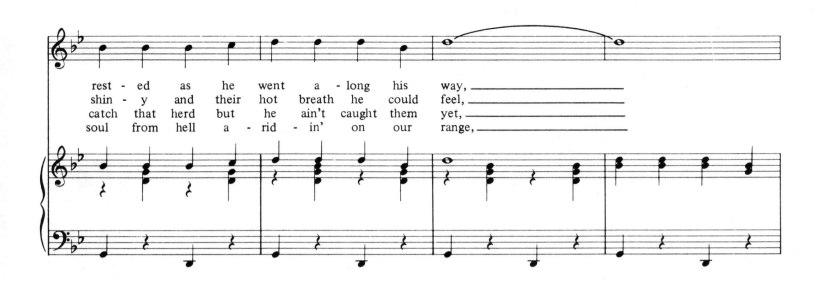

rest - ed   as   he   went   a - long   his   way, _____
shin - y   and   their   hot   breath   he   could   feel, _____
catch   that   herd   but   he   ain't   caught   them   yet, _____
soul   from   hell   a - rid - in'   on   our   range, _____

When   all   at   once   a   might - y   herd   of   red - eyed   cows   he
A   bolt   of   fear   went   through   him   as   they   thun - dered   thru   the
'Cause   they've   got   to   ride   for - ev - er   on   that   range   up   in   the
Then,   cow - boy,   change   your   ways   to - day   or   with   us   you   will

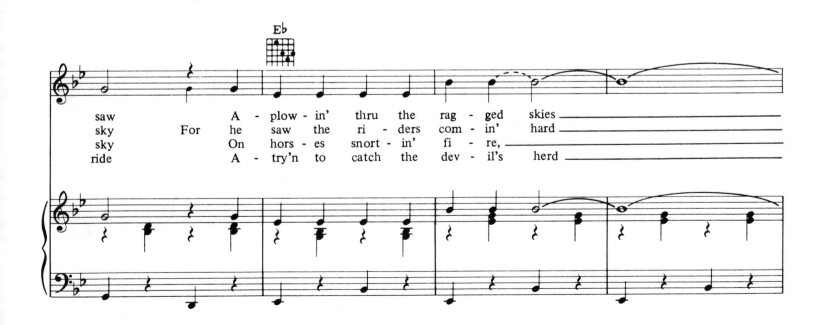

saw   A - plow - in'   thru   the   rag - ged   skies _____
sky   For   he   saw   the   ri - ders   com - in'   hard _____
sky   On   hors - es   snort - in'   fi - re, _____
ride   A - try'n   to   catch   the   dev - il's   herd _____

1950
Mona Lisa
from the Paramount Picture CAPTAIN CAREY, U.S.A.

Words and Music by JAY LIVINGSTON
and RAY EVANS

1951
Cry

Words and Music by
CHURCHILL KOHLMAN

Moderately with expression

If your sweet-heart sends a let-ter of good-bye, _____ It's no
se-cret you'll feel bet-ter if you cry _____ When wak-ing from a
bad dream don't you some-times think it's real? But it's on-ly false e-mo-tions that you

1952
Your Cheatin' Heart

Words and Music by
HANK WILLIAMS

1953
I Love Paris
from CAN-CAN

Words and Music by
COLE PORTER

Ev - 'ry time I look down on this time - less town, wheth - er blue or gray be her skies, wheth - er loud be her

cheers, or wheth - er soft be her tears, more and more

do I re - al - ize

Slow Fox Trot

I love Par - is in the spring - time, _____

I love Par - is in the fall, _____

I love Par-is in the win-ter when it driz-zles,

I love Par-is in the sum-mer when it siz-zles.

I love Par-is ev-'ry mo-ment, _____

ev-'ry mo-ment of the year. _____

1954
Shake, Rattle and Roll

Words and Music by
CHARLES CALHOUN

Verse 4

don't love me no more. I be-

lieve you're do-in' me wrong__ and now I know,__ I be-

lieve you're do-in' me wrong__ and now I know;__ The

more I work, the fast-er my mon-ey goes._____

D.S. al Fine
(3rd ending)

1955
Autumn Leaves
(Les Feuilles Mortes)

English lyric by JOHNNY MERCER
French lyric by JACQUES PREVERT
Music by JOSEPH KOSMA

Slowly, with much feeling

Oh! je vou-drais tant que tu te sou-viennes, des jours heu-reux où nous é -tions a -mis.
Les Feuil-les Mortes se ra-massent à la pelle, les sou - ve -nirs et les re-grets aus-si.

En ce temps-là la vie é -tait plus belle et le so - leil plus brû - lant qu'au-jourd'hui.
Mais mon a-mour si - len -cieux et fi - dèle sou - rit tou-jours et re - mer -cie la vie.

Les Feuil-les Mortes se ra-massent à la pelle, Tu vois, je n'ai pas ou - bli - é.
Je t'ai-mais tant, tu é - tais si jo - lie, Com - ment veux-tu que je t'ou - blie.

1956
The Great Pretender

Words and Music by
BUCK RAM

Lyrics:

Oh, yes__ I'm the great pre-tend-er,__ Pre-
tend-in' I'm__ do-in' well; My need is such,__ I pre-
tend too much, I'm lone-ly but no - one can tell. Oh,

heart _____ can't con-ceal; Oh, _____ yes, _____ I'm the great pre - tend - er, _____ Just

laugh - in' and gay _____ like a clown; I seem to be _____ what I'm

not, you see, I'm wear - in' my heart _____ like a crown; Pre -

tend - in' that you're _____ still a - roun'. Oh, roun'.

1957
All Shook Up

Words and Music by OTIS BLACKWELL
and ELVIS PRESLEY

Medium Shuffle

A - well - a, bless my soul, __ what's wrong with me? __ I'm

itch - ing like a man __ on a fuz - zy tree. __ My friends say I'm act - in'

queer as a bug, __ I'm in love! I'm all shook up! __ Mm __

1958
I Can't Stop Loving You

Words and Music by
DON GIBSON

time _____ heals ____ a bro - ken heart, _____

____ but time has stood still _____ since we've been a -

part. _____ I can't stop lov - ing you, _____
I can't stop lov - ing you, _____

____ so I've made up my mind _____ to live in
____ there's no use to try. _____ Pre - tend there's

1959
Kansas City

Words and Music by JERRY LEIBER
and MIKE STOLLER

F7

stand - in' on the cor - ner ___ Twelfth Street and Vine,
pack __ my clothes, _____ leave at the __ crack of dawn.

C

___ with my
___ My old

G7   F7

Kan - sas Cit - y ba - by and a bot - tle of Kan - sas __ Cit - y wine.
la - dy will be sleep - in' an' she won't know where I'm gone. __

C7

Well, __ I
'Cause if I

1960
If Ever I Would Leave You
from CAMELOT

Words by ALAN JAY LERNER
Music by FREDERICK LOEWE

1961
Runaway

Words and Music by DEL SHANNON
and MAX CROOK

1962
I Left My Heart in San Francisco

Words by DOUGLASS CROSS
Music by GEORGE CORY

1963
Our Day Will Come

Words by BOB HILLIARD
Music by MORT GARSON

MCA Music Publishing

1964
The Girl from Ipanema
(Garôta de Ipanema)

Music by ANTONIO CARLOS JOBIM
English Words by NORMAN GIMBEL
Original Words by VINICIUS DE MORAES

1965
Yesterday

Words and Music by JOHN LENNON
and PAUL McCARTNEY

Moderately, with expression

Yes-ter- day,___
Sud-den- ly,___ all my trou-bles seemed so
I'm not half the man___ I

far to a- way,___
used to be, Now it looks as though___ they're
There's a sha - dow hang - ing

1966
Monday, Monday

Words and Music by
JOHN PHILLIPS

MCA Music Publishing

1967
Happy Together

Words and Music by GARRY BONNER
and ALAN GORDON

I-mag-ine me and you,___ I do.   I   think a-bout you
call you up,___ in-vest a dime,   and you say you be-

day and night.___ It's on-ly right   to think a-bout the girl you love___ and hold her
long to me___ and ease my mind,   i-mag-ine how the world could be___ so ver-y

tight, so hap-py to-geth-er._____   If I should
fine, so hap-py to-

1968
Hey Jude

Words and Music by JOHN LENNON
and PAUL McCARTNEY

1969
Raindrops Keep Fallin' on My Head

Lyric by HAL DAVID
Music by BURT BACHARACH

1970
Your Song

Words and Music by ELTON JOHN
and BERNIE TAUPIN

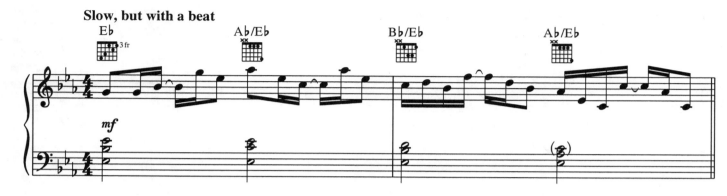

Slow, but with a beat

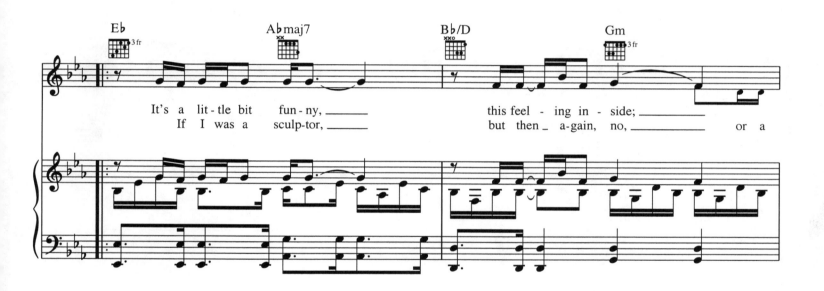

It's a lit-tle bit fun-ny,_____ this feel-ing in-side;_____
If I was a sculp-tor,_____ but then_ a-gain, no,_____ or a

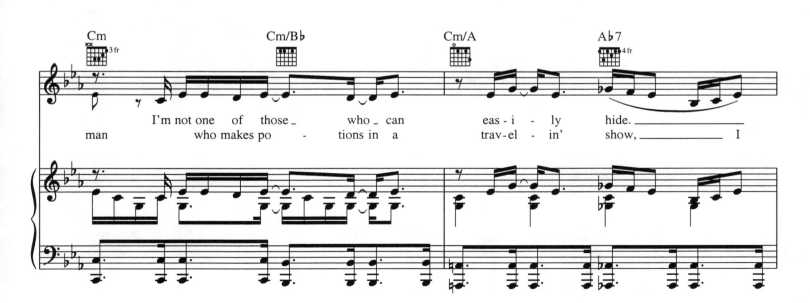

I'm not one of those_ who_ can eas-i-ly hide._____
man who makes po-tions in a trav-el-in' show,_____ I

1971
It's Too Late

Words by TONI STERN
Music by CAROLE KING

it, oh, ___ no, ___ no, ___ no, ___ no, ___ no, ___ no. ___

There'll be good times _ a-gain for me and _ you, _ but we just can't stay to-geth-er; don't you

1972
Rocky Mountain High

Words by JOHN DENVER
Music by JOHN DENVER and MIKE TAYLOR

1973
Killing Me Softly with His Song

Words by NORMAN GIMBEL
Music by CHARLES FOX

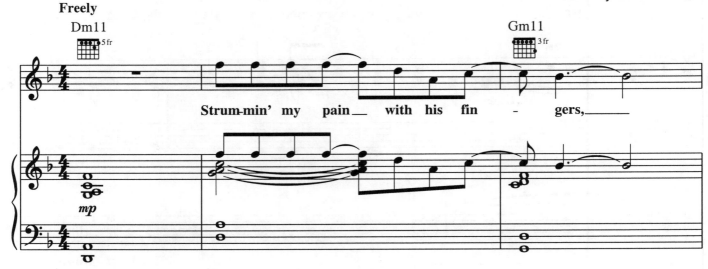

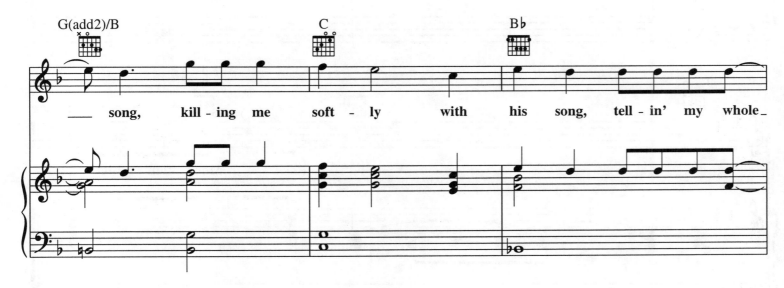

1974
Don't Let the Sun Go Down on Me

Words and Music by ELTON JOHN
and BERNIE TAUPIN

I'm _____ grow-ing tired _____ and time stands still be-fore_

_____ me. Fro-zen here, _

on the lad-der of___ my___ life.

1975
Can't Smile Without You

Words and Music by CHRIS ARNOLD,
DAVID MARTIN and GEOFF MORROW

1976
Tonight's the Night
(Gonna Be Alright)

Words and Music by
ROD STEWART

1977
How Deep Is Your Love
from the Motion Picture SATURDAY NIGHT FEVER

Words and Music by BARRY GIBB,
MAURICE GIBB and ROBIN GIBB

1978
Dust in the Wind

Words and Music by
KERRY LIVGREN

ev - 'ry - thing _ is dust in the wind.
wind.)

Repeat and Fade

Optional Ending

poco rit.

1979
Y.M.C.A.

Words and Music by JACQUES MORALI,
HENRI BELOLO and VICTOR WILLIS

1. Young man, there's no need to feel down. I said,
2., 3. *(See additional lyrics)*

Additional Lyrics

2. **Young man, are you listening to me?**
   I said, young man what do you want to be?
   I said, young man you can make real your dreams
   But you've got to know this one thing.

   No man does it all by himself.
   I said young man put your pride on the shelf.
   And just go there to the Y.M.C.A.
   I'm sure they can help you today.
   To Chorus:

3. **Young man, I was once in your shoes**
   I said, I was down and out and with the blues.
   I felt no man cared if I were alive.
   I felt the whole world was so jive.

   That's when someone come up to me
   And said, "Young man, take a walk up the street.
   It's a place there called the Y.M.C.A.
   They can start you back on your way."
   To Chorus:

1980
Sailing

Words and Music by
CHRISTOPHER CROSS

To Coda

1981
Physical

Words and Music by STEPHEN A. KIPNER
and TERRY SHADDICK

1982
Chariots of Fire
from CHARIOTS OF FIRE

Music by
VANGELIS

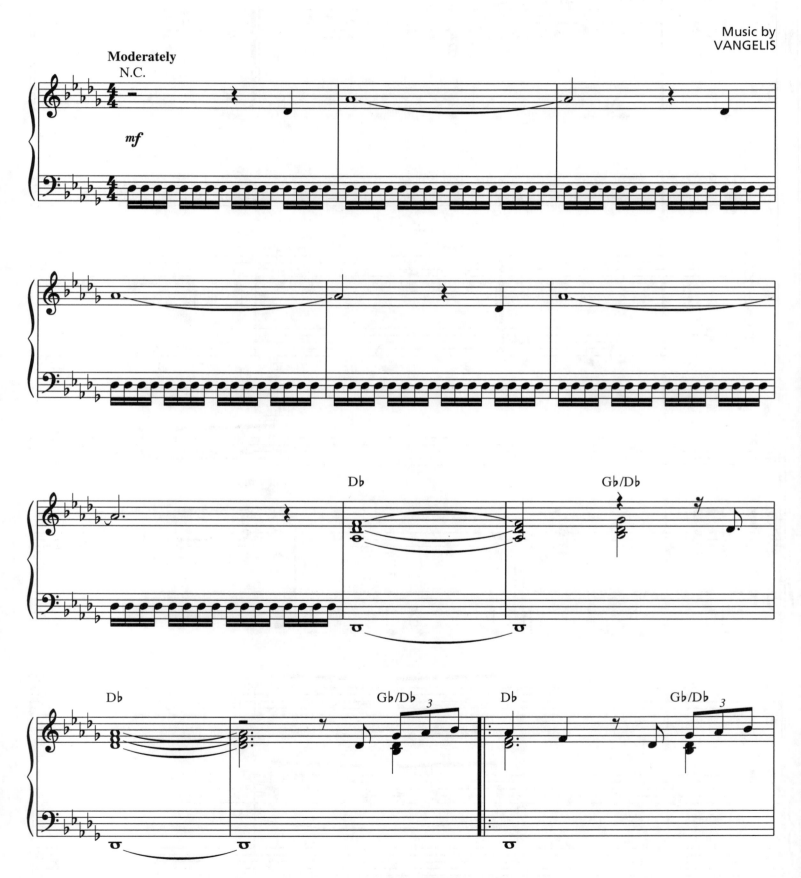

1983
Time After Time

Words and Music by CYNDI LAUPER
and ROB HYMAN

1984
I Just Called to Say I Love You

Words and Music by
STEVIE WONDER

1985

We Built This City

Words and Music by BERNIE TAUPIN, MARTIN PAGE,
DENNIS LAMBERT and PETER WOLF

Medium rock

We built this cit - y, we built this cit - y on

rock and __ roll. Built __ this cit - y, we built this cit - y on

rock and __ roll. __

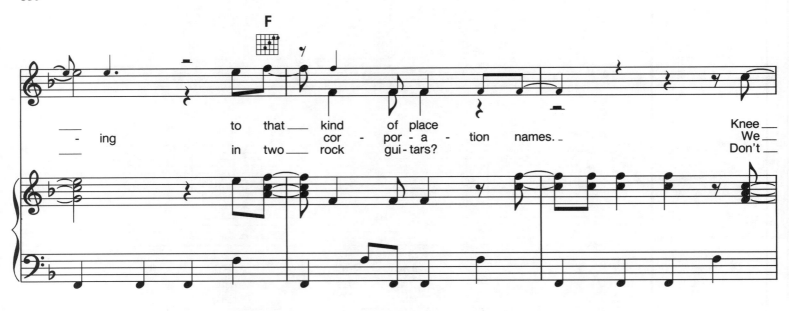

to that ___ kind of place
in two ___ rock gui - tars?
cor - por - a - tion names. ___
Knee ___
We ___
Don't ___

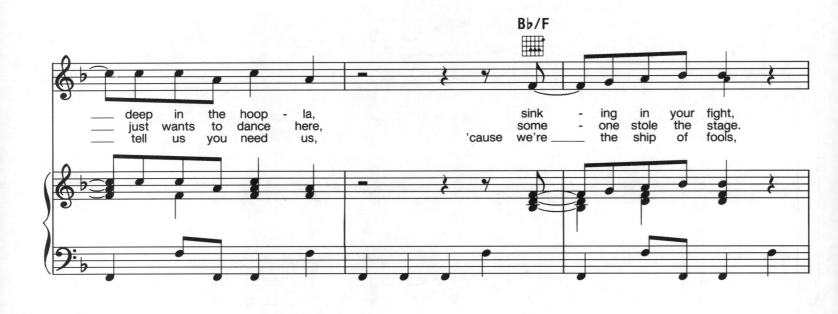

___ deep in the hoop - la,
___ just wants to dance here,
___ tell us you need us,
sink - ing in your fight,
some - one stole the stage.
'cause we're ___ the ship of fools,

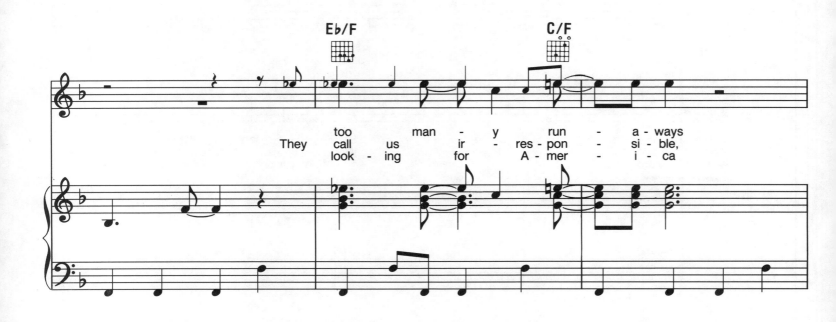

They call us ir - res - pon - si - ble,
look - ing for A - mer - i - ca
too man - y run - a - ways

1986
Glory of Love
Theme from KARATE KID PART II

Words and Music by DAVID FOSTER,
PETER CETERA and DIANE NINI

1987
I Still Haven't Found What I'm Looking For

Words by BONO
Music by U2

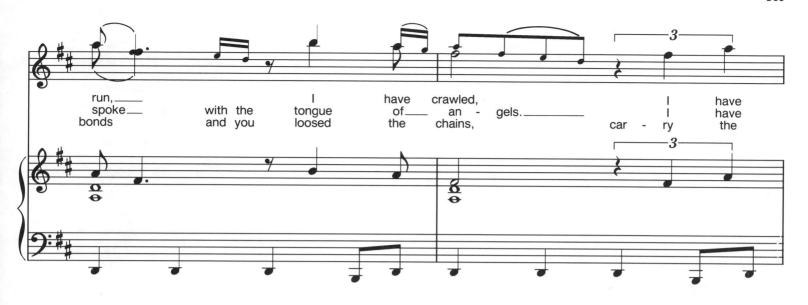

run,_____ I have crawled, I have
spoke_____ with the tongue of____ an - gels._____
bonds and you loosed the chains, car - ry have the

sealed_____ these these ci - ty walls,_____ these ci - ty
held the these hand of the dev - il. It was warm these ci
cross of my shame, of in my

Dsus/G

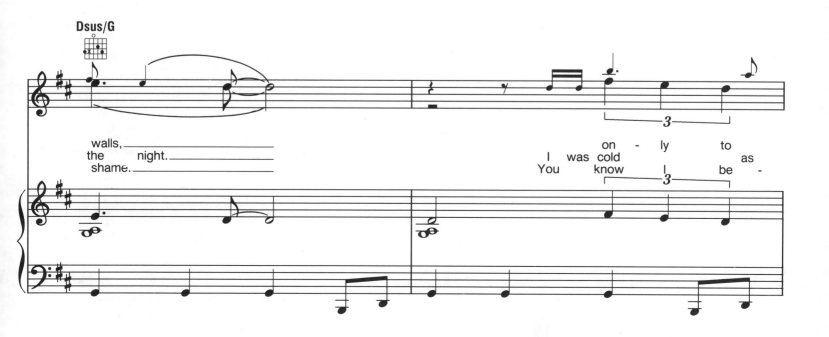

walls,_____ on - ly to
the night._____ I was cold as
shame._____ You know I be -

1988
Kokomo
from the Motion Picture COCKTAIL

Words and Music by MIKE LOVE, TERRY MELCHER,
JOHN PHILLIPS and SCOTT McKENZIE

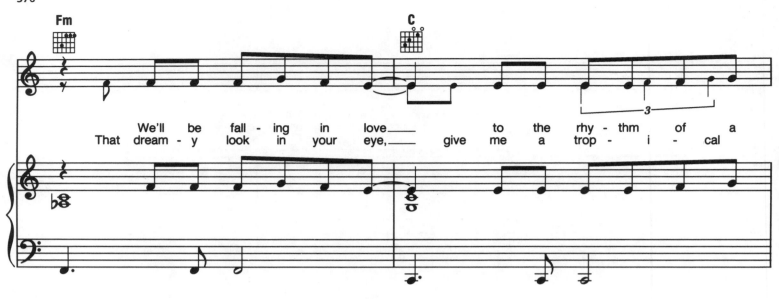

We'll be fall - ing in love____ to the rhy - thm of a
That dream - y look in your eye,____ give me a trop - i - cal

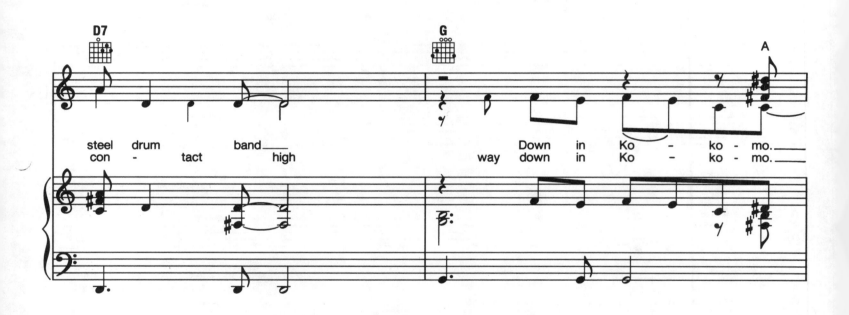

steel drum band____ Down in Ko - ko - mo.____
con - tact band high way down in Ko - ko - mo.____

ru - ba
Ja - mai - ca, oo____ I wan - na take you to Ber -

1989
Under the Sea
from Walt Disney's THE LITTLE MERMAID

Lyrics by HOWARD ASHMAN
Music by ALAN MENKEN

1990
How Am I Supposed to Live Without You

Words and Music by MICHAEL BOLTON
and DOUG JAMES

1991
Someday

Moderately, with a steady beat

Words and Music by MARIAH CAREY
and BEN MARGULIES

just think _ a - gain 'cause _ I won't need _ your _ love an - y -

more! _____

Some - day, _

1992
End of the Road
from the Paramount Motion Picture BOOMERANG

Words and Music by BABYFACE,
L.A. REID and DARYL SIMMONS

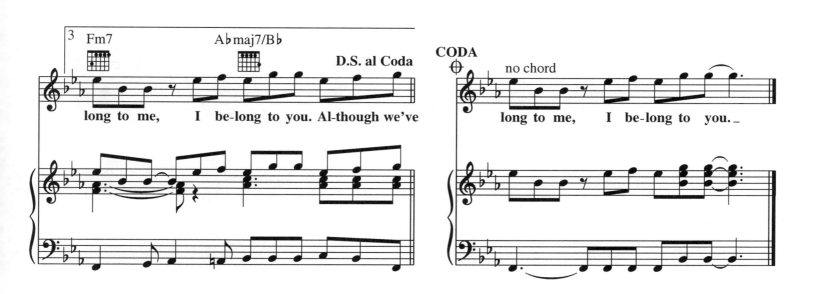

Additional Lyrics

(Spoken:) *Girl, I'm here for you.*
All those times at night when you just hurt me,
And just ran out with that other fellow,
Baby, I knew about it.
I just didn't care.
You just don't understand how much I love you, do you?
I'm here for you.
I'm not out to go out there and cheat all night just like you did, baby.
But that's alright, huh, I love you anyway.
And I'm still gonna be here for you 'til my dyin' day, baby.
Right now, I'm just in so much pain, baby.
'Cause you just won't come back to me, will you?
Just come back to me.

Yes, baby, my heart is lonely.
My heart hurts, baby, yes, I feel pain too.
Baby please...

1993
Fields of Gold

Written and Composed by
STING

1994
Can You Feel the Love Tonight
from Walt Disney Pictures' THE LION KING

Music by ELTON JOHN
Lyrics by TIM RICE

Pop Ballad

mp legato

With pedal

There's a calm __ sur-ren-der
There's a time __ for ev-'ry-one,

to the rush __ of day, __ when the heat __ of the roll-ing world __
if they on-ly learn __ that the twist-ing ka-lei-do-scope __

can be turned __ a-way. __ An en-chant-ed mo-ment,
moves us all ___ in turn. __ There's a rhyme __ and rea-son

1995
Exhale
(Shoop Shoop)
from the Original Soundtrack Album WAITING TO EXHALE

Words and Music by
BABYFACE

1996
I Finally Found Someone

from THE MIRROR HAS TWO FACES

Words and Music by BARBRA STREISAND, MARVIN HAMLISCH,
R.J. LANGE and BRYAN ADAMS

1997
Butterfly Kisses

Words and Music by RANDY THOMAS
and BOB CARLISLE

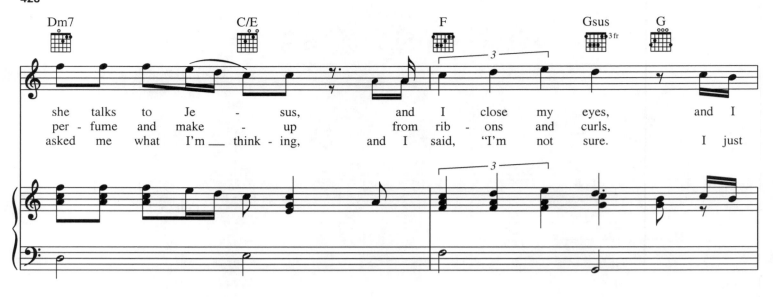

she talks to Je - sus, and I close my eyes, and I
per - fume and make - up from rib - ons and curls,
asked me what I'm __ think - ing, and I said, "I'm not sure. I just

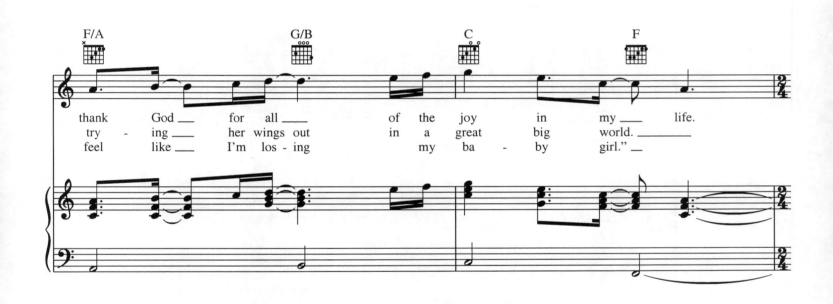

thank God __ for all __ of the joy in my __ life.
try - ing __ her wings out in a great big world. _____
feel like __ I'm los - ing my ba - by girl." __

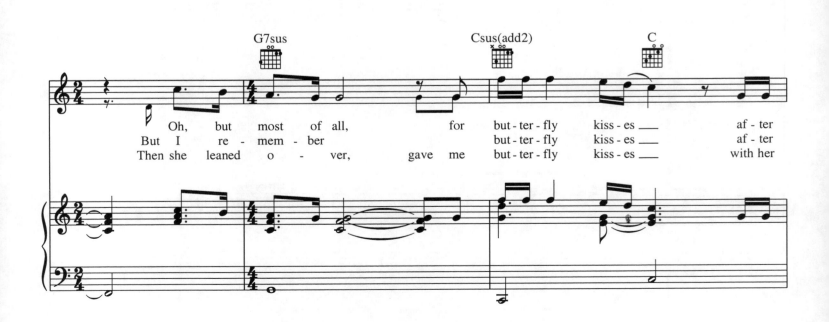

Oh, but most of all, for but - ter - fly kiss - es __ af - ter
But I re - mem - ber but - ter - fly kiss - es __ af - ter
Then she leaned o - ver, gave me but - ter - fly kiss - es __ with her

1998
You're Still the One

Words and Music by SHANIA TWAIN
and R.J. LANGE

1999
You'll Be in My Heart
(Pop Version)
from Walt Disney Pictures' TARZAN™

Words and Music by
PHIL COLLINS

be here in _____ my _ heart al - ways.

D.S. al Coda

CODA

Don't lis - ten to them, ___ 'cause you
des - ti - ny calls _ you you

what do they _ know?_ We need each oth - er to
must _ be _ strong. _ It may not be with you, but you've

What do they know? ___
Got - ta be strong. ___

BIG BOOKS OF MUSIC

Our "Big Books" feature big selections of popular titles under one cover, perfect for performing musicians, holiday sing-alongs, and music aficionados. All books are arranged for piano, voice, and guitar, and feature stay-open binding, so the books lie flat without breaking the spine.

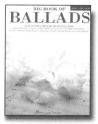

BIG BOOK OF BALLADS
63 SONGS.

00310485............$19.95

BIG BOOK OF CLASSICAL MUSIC
100 SONGS.

00310508............$19.95

BIG BOOK OF MOVIE MUSIC
72 SONGS.

00311582............$19.95

BIG BOOK OF BROADWAY
76 SONGS.

00311658............$19.95

BIG BOOK OF CONTEMPORARY CHRISTIAN FAVORITES
50 SONGS.

00310021............$19.95

THE BIG BOOK OF NOSTALGIA
158 SONGS.

00310004............$19.95

BIG BOOK OF CHILDREN'S SONGS
55 SONGS.

00359261............$12.95

BIG BOOK OF COUNTRY MUSIC
64 SONGS.

00310188............$19.95

BIG BOOK OF RHYTHM & BLUES
67 SONGS.

00310169............$19.95

GREAT BIG BOOK OF CHILDREN'S SONGS
76 SONGS.

00310002............$14.95

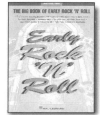

BIG BOOK OF EARLY ROCK N' ROLL
99 SONGS.

00310398............$19.95

BIG BOOK OF ROCK
78 SONGS.

00311566............$19.95

MIGHTY BIG BOOK OF CHILDREN'S SONGS
65 SONGS.

00310467............$14.95

BIG BOOK OF JAZZ
75 SONGS.

00311557............$19.95

BIG BOOK OF STANDARDS
86 SONGS.

00311667............$19.95

REALLY BIG BOOK OF CHILDREN'S SONGS
63 SONGS.

00310372............$15.95

BIG BOOK OF LATIN AMERICAN SONGS
89 SONGS.

00311562............$19.95

BIG BOOK OF SWING
84 SONGS.

00310359............$19.95

BIG BOOK OF CHRISTMAS SONGS
126 SONGS.

00311520............$19.95

BIG BOOK OF LOVE AND WEDDING SONGS
80 SONGS.

00311567............$19.95

BIG BOOK OF TV THEME SONGS
78 SONGS.

00310504............$19.95

FOR MORE INFORMATION, SEE YOUR LOCAL MUSIC DEALER,
OR WRITE TO:

Prices, contents, and availability subject to change without notice.

HAL•LEONARD®
CORPORATION
7777 W. BLUEMOUND RD. P.O. BOX 13819 MILWAUKEE, WI 53213

VISIT **halleonard.com** FOR OUR ENTIRE CATALOG
AND TO VIEW OUR COMPLETE SONGLISTS.

0699

Classic Collections Of Your Favorite Songs

arranged for piano, voice, and guitar.

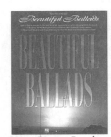

Beautiful Ballads

A massive collection of 87 songs, including: April In Paris • Autumn In New York • Call Me Irresponsible • Cry Me A River • I Wish You Love • I'll Be Seeing You • If • Imagine • Isn't It Romantic? • It's Impossible (Somos Novios) • Mona Lisa • Moon River • People • The Way We Were • A Whole New World (Aladdin's Theme) • and more.

00311679 ....$17.95

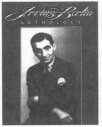

Irving Berlin Anthology

A comprehensive collection of 61 timeless songs with a bio, song background notes, and photos. Songs include: Always • Blue Skies • Cheek To Cheek • God Bless America • Marie • Puttin' On The Ritz • Steppin' Out With My Baby • There's No Business Like Show Business • White Christmas • (I Wonder Why?) You're Just In Love • and more.

00312493 ....$19.95

The Best Standards Ever Volume 1 (A-L)

72 beautiful ballads, including: All The Things You Are • Bewitched • Can't Help Lovin' Dat Man • Don't Get Around Much Anymore • Getting To Know You • God Bless' The Child • Hello, Young Lovers • I Got It Bad And That Ain't Good • It's Only A Paper Moon • I've Got You Under My Skin • The Lady Is A Tramp • Little White Lies.

00359231 ....$15.95

The Best Standards Ever Volume 2 (M-Z)

72 songs, including: Makin' Whoopee • Misty • Moonlight In Vermont • My Funny Valentine • Old Devil Moon • The Party's Over • People Will Say We're In Love • Smoke Gets In Your Eyes • Strangers In The Night • Tuxedo Junction • Yesterday.

00359232 ....$15.95

The Big Book of Standards

86 classics essential to any music library, including: April In Paris • Autumn In New York • Blue Skies • Cheek To Cheek • Heart And Soul • I Left My Heart In San Francisco • In The Mood • Isn't It Romantic? • Mona Lisa • Moon River • The Nearness Of You • Out Of Nowhere • Spanish Eyes • Star Dust • Stella By Starlight • That Old Black Magic • They Say It's Wonderful • What Now My Love • and more.

00311667 ....$19.95

Classic Jazz Standards

56 jazz essentials: All the Things You Are • Don't Get Around Much Anymore • How Deep Is the Ocean • In the Wee Small Hours of the Morning • Polka Dots and Moonbeams • Satin Doll • Skylark • Tangerine • Tenderly • What's New? • and more.

00310310 ....$16.95

I'll Be Seeing You: 50 Songs of World War II

A salute to the music and memories of WWII, including a year-by-year chronology of events on the homefront, dozens of photos, and 50 radio favorites of the GIs and their families back home, including: Boogie Woogie Bugle Boy • Don't Sit Under The Apple Tree (With Anyone Else But Me) • I Don't Want To Walk Without You • I'll Be Seeing You • Moonlight In Vermont • There's A Star-Spangled Banner Waving Somewhere • You'd Be So Nice To Come Home To • and more.

00311698 ....$19.95

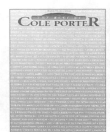

Best of Cole Porter

38 of his classics, including: All Of You • Anything Goes • Be A Clown • Don't Fence Me In • I Get A Kick Out Of You • In The Still Of The Night • Let's Do It (Let's Fall In Love) • Night And Day • You Do Something To Me • and many

00311577 ....$14.95

Big Band Favorites

A great collection of 70 of the best Swing Era songs, including: East of the Sun • Honeysuckle Rose • I Can't Get Started with You • I'll Be Seeing You • In the Mood • Let's Get Away from It All • Moonglow • Moonlight in Vermont • Opus One • Stompin' at the Savoy • Tuxedo Junction • more!

00310445 ....$16.95

The Best of Rodgers & Hammerstein

A capsule of 26 classics from this legendary duo. Songs include: Climb Ev'ry Mountain • Edelweiss • Getting To Know You • I'm Gonna Wash That Man Right Outa My Hair • My Favorite Things • Oklahoma • The Surrey With The Fringe On Top • You'll Never Walk Alone • and more.

00308210 ....$12.95

The Best Songs Ever

80 must-own classics, including: All I Ask Of You • Body And Soul • Crazy • Endless Love • Fly Me To The Moon • Here's That Rainy Day • In The Mood • Love Me Tender • Memory • Moonlight In Vermont • My Funny Valentine • People • Satin Doll • Save The Best For Last • Somewhere Out There • Strangers In The Night • Tears In Heaven • A Time For Us • The Way We Were • When I Fall In Love • You Needed Me • and more.

00359224 .... $19.95

Torch Songs

Sing your heart out with this collection of 59 sultry jazz and big band melancholy masterpieces, including: Angel Eyes • Cry Me A River • I Can't Get Started • I Got It Bad And That Ain't Good • I'm Glad There Is You • Lover Man (Oh, Where Can You Be?) • Misty • My Funny Valentine • Stormy Weather • and many more! 224 pages.

00490446 ....$16.95

0899